# Celtic Flame

# Celtic Flame

------------------------→

An Insider's Guide to Irish Pagan Tradition

Aedh Rua

iUniverse, Inc.
New York  Bloomington

# Celtic Flame
## An Insider's Guide to Irish Pagan Tradition

Copyright © 2008 by Aedh Rua

All rights reserved. No part of this book may be used or reproduced by any means, graphic, electronic, or mechanical, including photocopying, recording, taping or by any information storage retrieval system without the written permission of the publisher except in the case of brief quotations embodied in critical articles and reviews.

This book is a work of non-fiction.
Names and places have been changed to protect the privacy of all individuals.
The events and situations are true.

iUniverse books may be ordered through booksellers or by contacting:

iUniverse
1663 Liberty Drive
Bloomington, IN 47403
www.iuniverse.com
1-800-Authors (1-800-288-4677)

Because of the dynamic nature of the Internet, any Web addresses or links contained in this book may have changed since publication and may no longer be valid. The views expressed in this work are solely those of the author and do not necessarily reflect the views of the publisher, and the publisher hereby disclaims any responsibility for them.

ISBN: 978-0-595-52970-4 (pbk)
ISBN: 978-0-595-63023-3 (EBK)

Printed in the United States of America

# *Acknowledgements*

A project like this could not come to fruition without the help of many people, both as sources of information, as critics and advisors, and as providers of moral support.

So, in no particular order:

Thanks are due to Kym ni Deoireann, and Kathryn Price for their support and advise through the many delays and revisions this manuscript has undergone. Thanks to Erynn Laurie for many interesting ideas and suggestions.

Thanks to Lynn Hudson, Desi Bergeron, and Kim Barnewold, all of whom were among the very first people to see me doing reconstructionist Celtic rituals, back in 1991. Thanks also to Kelly Woodruff, for typing the very first Celtic Outline, the earliest ancestor of this book, back in 1992. Thanks to Rachel Gold, who worked with me to create an early version of my Irish Pagan practice between 1993 and 1995. Thanks are also due to Carole Rogan, for moral support and love during the years from 1994 to 2004, and also for the fantastic rituals we did together in the mid-90s. Dave Schaal has been a constant source of support, ideas, and occasionally texts, and I cannot thank him enough. Thanks also to Chad McAnally, and Cindy Miller, for their dedication to my vision.

Candace Olson, Frank Joyce, and the late Sean T. Kelly are responsible for much of the state of my Irish. Additionally, I must thank the staff of Irish Books and Media, in Minneapolis, who started me out with Buntús Cainte, my first Irish course, all those years ago. Thanks are due to Chris

Gwinn, Antonio Tolosa-Leal, and Alexei Kondratiev for my understanding of Continental Celtic languages. Also I must thank John Koch and the staff of the University of Wales Center for Advanced Welsh and Celtic Studies, whose Old Common Celtic Lexicon has been greatly useful in understanding the roots of the Celtic languages, and the proto-Celtic vocabulary.

Many scholars and Celticists have influenced my work. I can only thank the most important of these. Alexei Kondratiev has provided the largest single contribution to my work, although it is in many ways coming to diverge from his own. Without his influence, this book would be in many ways much the poorer. Georges Dumezil is also a critical influence, without which this book would have been unrecognizable, probably impossible. Bruce Lincoln has greatly expanded my understanding of various aspects of cosmology, and his influence is visible in many parts of this text. Alwin and Brinley Rees have also greatly influenced my understanding of early Celtic cosmology and ideology. Again, this book would not have been written without their work as a partial basis. Sean O'Tuathail has also provided much of the ideology embodied in this work. While my book would exist without him, it would be much poorer without his influence. Likewise, Michael Enright has provided the basis for much of my understanding of the complex of ideas surrounding sovereignty in Celtic cultures. His influence lies behind the scenes, so far as this text is concerned, but is no less important for that. Katherine Briggs provides many of my ideas on the nature of the Fair Folk, and their various divisions, without which I would much less about an important element of the older Gaelic religion. Nerys Patterson and Raimund Karl are my main sources on old Irish law and society, along with lesser, but still significant, influences from Michael Newton, Patrick Weston Joyce, and Michael Richter. Alexander Carmichael's *Carmina Gadelica* has been the most important source of my ritual poetry and incantations, and Kevin Dánaher's *The Year in Ireland* for holiday lore. The works of Daragh Smyth and James Mackillop have provided me with invaluable reference works, while the work of Angelica Gulermovich Epstein and Rosalind Clark has greatly influenced my ideas on Irish Goddesses.

In addition to all the above, many others have influenced my work in various small ways. To all of them, too, I owe thanks.

# Table of Contents

| | | |
|---|---|---|
| I. | Introduction | ix |
| II. | Chapter 1: an enduring tradition | 1 |
| III. | Chapter 2: Gods and Spirits | 7 |
| | A. The Tuatha Dé Danann | 7 |
| |    1. Déithe Adhartha | 10 |
| |    2. Déithe Danann | 26 |
| |    3. Éarlaimh | 28 |
| | C. The Daoine Sídhe | 38 |
| |    1. Their Nature | 38 |
| |    2. Types of Daoine Sídhe | 40 |
| IV. | Chapter 3: Fírinne | 45 |
| | A. Dlúth, Dán, and Slí | 46 |
| | B. Ethics and Virtues | 46 |
| | C. Oineach and Bua | 49 |
| | D. Gessa | 50 |
| | E. Nascmhíol, Beirmhíol, and Claenmhíol | 51 |
| | F. The Tuath Concept | 54 |
| | G. Divisions of a Tuath | 55 |
| | H. Oineach in the Tuath | 56 |
| | I. Céilsine | 59 |
| | J. Lánamnas | 61 |
| | K. Altramas | 63 |
| | L. The Fénechas | 63 |
| V. | Chapter 4: The Otherworld | 67 |
| | A. The Journey to the Otherworld | 68 |
| | B. The Nature of the Otherworld | 70 |
| VI. | Chapter 5: The Fomoire | 75 |
| | B. Types of Fomoire | 77 |

| | | |
|---|---|---|
| | C. Protection against the Fomoire ...............................................80 | |
| VII. | **Chapter 6: Íobairt .................................................................. 85** | |
| | A. The Neimheadh as a place of worship .....................................86 | |
| | B. Cleathansaí – Tools and Gear...................................................88 | |
| | C. Daily Prayers ...........................................................................91 | |
| | D. The Basic Ritual.....................................................................94 | |
| | E. Holidays, Rituals, and the Sacred Year ....................................97 | |
| VIII. | **Chapter 7: Death and the Dead............................................. 109** | |
| | A. Forms of Afterlife..................................................................109 | |
| | B. Interactions with the Dead ...................................................111 | |
| | C. Death Omens .......................................................................112 | |
| IX. | **Appendix A: The Basic Ritual in Irish ................................... 121** | |
| X. | **Appendix B:  Invocations in Irish and English ...................... 123** | |
| XI. | **Appendix C:  Celtic Reconstructionist Organizations, Websites and Leaders ............................................................................ 133** | |
| XII. | **Appendix D: Language Learning Resources and Celtic Websites ................................................................................. 135** | |
| XIII. | **Notes ..................................................................................... 138** | |
| XIV. | **Bibliography ......................................................................... 152** | |

# Introduction

Celtic Paganism is a hot topic these days. You hear it discussed endlessly in Pagan chatrooms, in egroups, on Witchvox, in generic books on Paganism, at Pagan Pride, and at Gatherings. It seems like every other Pagan is a Celtic Pagan, proud of their Irish, Scots, Scots-Irish, or Welsh heritage.

Despite all the interest, good information on the topic is pretty hard to get. Most books on Celtic traditions just scratch the surface, and almost none explore the topic in its proper cultural context. While there seems to be an awful lot of people who want to practice a deeper and more authentic Celtic spirituality, most of them have no idea where to go for answers, and, when they do, they often find the amount of work they have to do, even just to start out, is intimidating, to say the least.

This books aims to solve that problem, at least as far as one book can.

**Celtic Flame** is an introduction to Irish Paganism as I have practiced it. It is a distillation of my twenty years of trying to reconstruct Celtic Paganism as authentically as possible, and of much knowledge from some of the best available sources. It will allow you, its reader, to have good, solid, accurate information on the Gods, on the various other types of spirit out there, on one version of Irish Pagan cosmology, worldview, ethics, values, and institutions. Even better, it should enable the ordinary reader, with no previous experience, to pick up the book, study it, and start performing reasonably authentic Gaelic rituals that work. It will let you worship the Gods and celebrate the major holidays, all the while knowing more-or-less what you are doing. And, it will give you suggestions for where to go for more and more advanced knowledge.

In short, this book can serve as your gateway to a more authentic and meaningful Pagan Celtic spiritual path.

It has been a long time in the coming. The first discussions on how to do a really **Celtic** version of Celtic Paganism date back to 1985, mostly at Pagan Spirit Gathering that year. I know 'cause I was there, along with a grab bag of folks who have gone their own ways over the years since: Murtagh Adamh an Doile, Kathryn Price NicDhàna, Ian Corrigan, Isaac Bonewits, and others. Those discussions weren't the beginning of Celtic Paganism, but they planted seed that would develop in many different directions in the years to follow.

The next year, at Pagan Spirit Gathering 1986, I taught a class in Celtic Paganism that was fairly well attended. Although quite rudimentary by my current standards, it was probably the best class of its kind that had been taught at PSG up to that point, and a major step for me toward a more meaningful spiritual practice. At about the same time, 1985 and 1986, I joined the neo-Druid group Ar nDraiocht Fein, though college kept me from devoting significant time to it.

For several years, I was too busy with graduate school to do much with Celtic spirituality. Starting in about 1990, though, I began once again to work on my spiritual path, doing research and discovering concepts that would become part of my practice in the years to come. When my library career took me to New Orleans in 1991-1992, I got some friends together and we experimented with some of the first reconstructed Celtic rituals I had ever done. When my career took me to Ohio, in 1992-1993, I worked with different friends to refine and develop things further. It was at this time that I wrote, and my friend Kelly Woodruff helped type, organize, and collate the very first Celtic Outline, the earliest ancestor to this book.

From 1993 to 1998, my career took me back to my home state of Minnesota. Here, I became involved with Carole Rogan, and we began doing Celtic rituals on her land in the North Woods, starting in 1994. At about the same time, I began working with a group of young students and alums of my own undergraduate school, Macalester College, to develop a more authentic version of Celtic Paganism. My friend Rachel Gold was particular assistance in this regard; I still use invocations written in the format she devised.

While all of this was going on, I made contact with the neo-Druid group Keltria, meeting with a couple of groves from time to time, and writing a couple articles for their magazine. From about 1993 to about 1995 there was much debate in Keltria about what qualified as "Celtic", and who could call themselves such. It was as a part of this debate that Alexei Kondratiev wrote his famous "Celt?" letter that has been reprinted on so many websites since. I also met Ellen Evert Hopman through Keltria. Ellen has gone on to write several books and found the Order of the Whiteoak, one of the most high-minded and authentic of neo-Druid groups.

The fruit of my work in those years was an unpublished book called *Walking with the Gods,* which I finished in 1996, and still have in my possession. Much of the material in this book is in fact taken from that one, including much of the material on deities, almost the entire Otherworld chapter, and much of the chapter on death and the dead.

In about 1995 or 1996, I discovered the website of the Celtic Reconstructionist group Imbas, and joined the group right away. I was much influenced by what I discovered through Imbas, and in their journal *An Tribhis Mór,* though I was otherwise not an especially active member.

Imbas had split off from the Nemeton list, which was the creation of Erynn Rowan Laurie. In about 1992, discussions began on PODS-net among Erynn, John Machate, and others. Erynn was a student of the legendary Sean Ó Tuathail, and was developing her own school of **filíocht**. The PODS-net discussions evolved into the Nemeton list, which became very well respected. In about 1994, Alexei Kondratiev, already active in the Celtic League American Branch, joined Nemeton. His posts have become immensely important to my own practice, forming the basis for my systems of theology and ethics, as one can see in chapters on these subjects.

From 1998-2001, my career took me back to Illinois, where I had already attended library school. Because this was my first library directorship, I had very little time to devote to my spiritual life. I did, however, correspond with Kym ni Deorainn, who was in those days head of the Aisling Association of Celtic Tribes.

In the early 1990s, Kym had been working with Kathryn Price NicDhána, whom I had met back at PSG 1985, to develop their Celtic paths further. Among other things, the two of them coined the term "Celtic Reconstructionism", first used by Kym in an article about 1992. Kathryn discovered the Nemeton list in 1994. I discovered Kym, and rediscovered Kathryn, about 1998. From 1998-2004, we were quite close, and I was an active member of their circle of Celtic Reconstructionists, though I no longer call myself a Celtic Reconstructionist today, for a wide variety of reasons.

In 2001, my career took me to Wisconsin, where I had earlier gone to graduate school, for another library directorship. Here, I organized a tuath for a couple of years, teaching students and preparing class materials. The basis for these class materials was found in a mixture of *Walking with the Gods,* the old Celtic Outline, some materials from my work with Rachel and the Mac students, various influences from Alexei Kondratiev's Nemeton posts, and correspondence with Kym and Kathryn. These class materials then formed the basis for this book, fleshed out with more material from *Walking with the Gods*, as well as plenty of new research and material.

The first draft of this book was finished in 2004, then set aside as my career and a relationship took me south to Florida. In 2007, I took it up again, and began refining, rewriting, and double-checking it. Now, at long last, it is finally ready, and I can present it to you.

Áedh Rua
Deerhaven, Florida
June, 2008

# 1
# A Living Tradition

This book is an introduction to Irish Paganism as I have practiced it for 20 years and more. Anyone reading it will have access to one, fully authentic interpretation of Irish Paganism, which will allow a way to enter this growing movement and to practice this religion. Those with an interest in Celtic mythology and religion who do not want to practice it will still find this book a very useful source of good, solid, authentic information about Pagan Irish culture and religion.

My own version of Irish Paganism, which differs from the versions created by others, just as theirs differ from one another, has a number of elements, among them:

1. Belief in the Tuatha Dé Danann Danann, the divine race of ancient Ireland.
2. Belief in the Otherworld, the home of the Gods and blessed dead.
3. The cosmic and social order of Fírinne, which embodies much of what modern Americans and Europeans might describe as Gaelic ethics, values, and culture.
4. A collection of ritual observances, holidays, and rites of passage.
5. Lore on the Fomoire, the foes of the Tuatha Dé Danann, and on the cosmic conflict between the divine and demonic races.
6. A body of lore on death, the dead, and the fate of the soul.

These basics, discussed in this book, do not begin to exhaust the richness of the Gaelic tradition, however. In addition, there are other elements, disciplines and bodies of lore, among them:

1. The body of lore dealing with magical poetry, divination, states of consciousness, assorted magical arts, meditation, and so on known as Draíocht.
2. A related body of lore dealing with poetry, inspiration, divination, the Oghams, and related topics, which we may call by the name Filíocht, or Filidecht.
3. A wide variety of warrior traditions, martial arts, and warrior disciplines, ranging from the Scottish "Cateran" styles of bladed combat, through Irish stick fighting, to the spiritual and mental disciplines of the warrior. These traditions are by no means exclusively Pagan, though they are mostly so.
4. The vast, and very much living tradition of Irish and Scottish music, as practiced in almost every major city in North America and the British Isles. Celtic music, of course, is more Christian than Pagan, and a part of the Gaelic inheritance s a whole.
5. The traditions of the Irish, Scots Gaelic, and Manx languages and literatures. These are also still living, indeed, struggling for survival, and need the support of people everywhere if they are to continue. They include some of the oldest and finest poetry and writing in Europe, and deserve to be kept alive. The understanding of the language, moreover, is essential to the Gaelic identity, and to the proper understanding of the old traditions, whether the Pagan traditions, or those of Celtic Christianity.
6. Irish and Scottish folk dance, another still living tradition, which is again found throughout the world. These traditions are, again, part of the greater Gaelic inheritance, and not at all exclusively Pagan.
7. A vast corpus of traditional arts and crafts, most without any particular religious foundation, but essential to the Gaelic way of life in earlier times. These include methods of building houses, spinning, weaving, carving, making furniture and other items, cooking, preserving food, farming, stock raising, and many other similar tasks. They are, of course, of little practical value in the modern world, but deserve continued life as a part of the Gaelic heritage.

This book correctly refers to only those elements of the broader Gaelic tradition that are purely Pagan and predominantly religious. It is, however, firmly rooted in Gaelic culture as a whole, and cannot be said to exist or be legitimate apart from that context.

**What are the sources of Irish Paganism?:** "So", a perceptive reader might ask, "where do you get this stuff? How do I know it's for real?" Indeed, an intelligent reader needs to ask this, because there is a lot of bad information out there. Unfortunately, Celtic Culture has become a very popular fad, with lots of clever and unscrupulous people rushing to take advantage of it. There is a lot of false and misleading material in print, much fakery and nonsense masquerading as legitimate Celtic Culture. So, how does one recognize the real thing, and tell it from the imitation? There are a number of ways. One, applicable to spiritual and religious issues is to consider the sources from which the writer gets his or her material. A legitimate version of the Gaelic religion will come from most or all of the following:

1. The early Irish vernacular texts, including such documents as the *Lebor Gabala h'Érenn, Cath Mag Tuired, Dindsenchus,* and the *Táin Bo Cualigne,* among a number of others. These texts are the legitimate written sources of early Irish lore and mythology. They are, in most cases, the earliest reliable information on the subject. They form the bedrock on which modern Irish Paganism is founded. Despite this, we must use these texts with caution. All of them were written after the introduction of Christianity, though some were written at a time when Pagan worship was still going on. Moreover, they were written by Christian scribes who were intent on adapting the ancient myths, the source of the foundations of early Irish society, including art, music, poetry, law, genealogy, land tenure, and so on, to a Christian milieu. This was needed in order to prevent Christianization from resulting in the disintegration of Irish society. In addition, the early scribes, who were familiar with Greco-Roman literature, wished to create native Irish epics to rival the Iliad and Odyssey. As a result, the vernacular texts alter and rearrange the myths from their original, Pagan forms. When using them, this must be remembered, and taken into account.
2. The folklore of the Gaelic peoples, as it has survived into recent times. The introduction of Christianity did not mean the end of the Pagan religion, which survived quite openly for a very long time. Indeed, it took centuries to build up a cadre of trained priests and monks able to take Christianity to the more remote parts of the country. Open Pagan worship was fully legal until at least 700 CE, and persisted for hundreds of years after that. Even when the country people had fully accepted Christianity, they adapted it to their own needs, and continued to believe in hosts of native spirits which

they continued to worship down to the present day. As a result, a vast body of lore has survived as part of Irish and Scottish folklore, including various forms of "fairy lore", holidays, traditional charms, healings, spells, prayers, values, customs, and so on. This material has been collected in various works, among them Carmichael's *Carmina Gadelica*, MacNeil's *The Festival of Lughnasadh*, McNeill's *Silver Bough*, Newton's *Handbook of the Scottish Gaelic World*, and Evans-Wentz's *Fairy-Faith in Celtic Countries*, among many other such works. They supply both the background of the spirit of the native culture and lore, and a useful corrective to some of the scribal alterations in the vernacular texts.

3. The traditions of mysticism in the Gaelic world, and the writings of mostly modern, but native, mystics. While such people as AE, or William Sharp, or Yeats, or, most recently, Sean O'Tuathail, are heavily influenced by Anglo-American ideas and culture, as well as syncretic movements such as Theosophy, they are still a continuing native tradition of mysticism and direct contact with the divine. The same goes for native traditions of Christian devotion and worship. All such traditions must be treated with the greatest caution, but may nonetheless be useful. Moreover, what is quickly discovered by the study of such traditions, is that the Tuatha Dé Danann are far from dead, but continue to interact with human beings down to the present day. Such contact can indeed provide us with a near-direct access to spiritual truth, *but only if such revelations are seen in the context of the Gaelic cultures, and checked against other traditions for accuracy.*

4. The findings of archaeologists can also shed light on the native traditions, and show us much about where the vernacular texts or oral traditions are accurate or not accurate. As such, archaeological findings can serve as a check on other sorts of sources, as well as a source of information in themselves. However, it must be emphasized that archaeologists are not able to determine the cultural, historical, or ideological contexts of their finds. Ideas cannot be preserved unless written down. Consequently, archaeological findings must always be understood *in the context of the culture and tradition as a whole.* Only thus may such findings be rendered meaningful, whether as a corrective for decayed aspects of the current traditions, or as a confirmation of those aspects still in touch with the deepest wellsprings of the Gaelic heritage.

5. The work of scholars in Indo-European studies, and in other, related cultures may also shed light on Gaelic traditions. Here, again, how-

ever, there are cautions. While Indo-European studies may show us the linguistic origin of a word, or the persistence of a practice among other similar and related societies, it cannot, again, make that information meaningful by itself. Once again, *this information must be compared to the Seanchas (tradition, lore) as it exists in native sources.* Only in this way can we see how, or if, the native, Gaelic tradition used one or another element of a putative Indo-European inheritance. One must also recognize that Indo-European studies are *highly theoretical and open to multiple interpretations.* They can give nothing like certainty.

6. Still less reliable are the accounts of Greco-Roman writers on their Celtic neighbors. These are really not accounts of Gaelic societies at all, but of other, very closely related, Continental and British Celtic cultures, from centuries in the past of even the earliest recorded Gaelic culture. Moreover, they are accounts written by foreign observers who have nothing resembling objectivity, indeed are often hostile to those they observe, and use nothing remotely like sound scholarly methods. Despite this, they are occasionally valuable, as eye-witness accounts of the behavior and customs of at least one Pagan Celtic people.

7. Finally, we can and do interact directly with the Tuatha Dé Danann, and may at times receive ideas, inspirations, interpretations, and guidance from them. *Such direct divine guidance must always be checked against the Seanchas as we have it.* Only if it does not conflict with the tradition, or, better, if it is confirmed by a fact previously unknown, can such revelations be accepted. Such divine guidance is not something limited to a few prophets or chosen leaders, but is freely available to all who interact with the Tuatha Dé Danann, provided they learn the traditions well enough to check their facts, and that they learn the language, so that such revelations may be understood in context. Without such divine guidance, no true revival of the old Gaelic religion would be possible. However, many modern revivalists have such guidance, which has often led them to reach the same conclusions by very different routes.

**The Irish Pagan Worldview:** Irish Paganism pictures the world as alive from end to end. Nature is not a dead collection of objects, but is instead filled with spirits, many of which are able to interact with humankind. Every tree, rock, hill, stream or other natural feature is home to a spirit. Every art or craft, every occupation has its divine patron, who will give information or answer prayers related to that occupation. Every mountain, river, forest, and region has its divine patron, who is concerned with the welfare of that area. Families, tribes, and nations also have divine patrons, as well as the living spirits of their ancestors, who watch over them and guide them. Over all the world reign the greater Gods, immortal, ancient, and mighty beings of light who war against the demons of the darkness.

The cosmos of Celtic Paganism is not the empty valueless world of modern materialism. In my version of Irish Paganism, all things have a spiritual essence, and a destiny that they must fulfill. Discovering and fulfilling this destiny is one of the great tasks of human life, and holds untold rewards. This spiritual essence gives rise to ritual prohibitions called **Gessa**, and to particular relationships with animal spirits. The world is filled with a surging spiritual power that may be tapped by those who know how, and used for magic, or just to bring victory and strength. This power is increased by keeping to a strict code of ethics and honor, which is also a part of the cosmic order, and governs the moral realm just as the laws of physics govern the physical world.

Pagan traditions also govern human society, promoting a way of life at once more natural, more meaningful, and more humane than that of the modern West. The structure of society is tribal, giving everyone a real sense of belonging to something greater than them. It is designed to live in harmony with the land, to be sustainable, and spiritually connected to the living Earth. It is designed to offer a place for everyone, to leave no one behind. It supports the rights of women, and offers meaningful and useful improvements to the institution of marriage, making marriage at once more equal, and more practical. The ancient Irish Pagan laws are humane and yet effective, working by the law of compensation, which rights wrongs, rather than merely making the offender suffer.

In these ways and many others Irish Paganism has much to offer the modern or post-modern world. It is simple enough to understand, yet rich enough to promote spiritual growth. It is well-founded and believable. It is backed by an entire culture that is compatible with the deepest and best impulses of modern culture, while correcting for its flaws. It promotes a deeply fulfilling and viable way of life. In all these ways it is positioned as a religion of the future, as well as a religion from the ancient past. It is truly an ancient but still living, vital tradition.

# 2

# Gods and Spirits

## Section 1: The Tuatha Dé Danann

The center of ancient Irish religion, and also the starting point, are the Tuatha Dé Danann. The term Tuatha Dé Danann actually translates as "Tribes of the Gods of Dánu", or perhaps as "Tribes of the Gods of Arts". It refers to a race of beings, essentially beings of light, or energy, who to some extent inhabit the natural world, indeed, precede humanity as the inhabitants of the Earth, and are of great power and wisdom. The Tuatha Dé Danann are only one of several divine races that have inhabited this world at various times. Others include the enigmatic Fir Bolgs, and the dreaded Fomoire.

The Tuatha Dé Danann are referred to in the ancient Irish texts as *De ocus an-de*, which we would render into modern Irish as *Déithe agus an-Déithe*, and which translates as "Gods and Not-Gods". The idea here is that the Tuatha Dé Danann include both the powerful deities and less powerful local land-spirits. Indeed, as we shall see there are various gradations of power and authority among the Tuatha Dé Danann, as in any human society.

The old traditions are reasonably clear on what the Tuatha Dé Danann are like, and later seers have done much to fill in any gaps in the picture. They are, then, beings of energy, naturally bodiless, unless they wish to take form. When they do take form, they tend to resemble a tall, shining humanoid figure, usually of great beauty, though there are many exceptions. The powers of the Tuatha Dé Danann vary greatly, from the greatest among them, who can control weather, disease, and the fortunes of nations, to the least, who can perhaps send good or ill luck. All of the Tuatha Dé Danann are immortal unless killed, and do not age, or, more accurately, may appear as any age they wish. The greatest among them may have aspects of them that are somewhat different from the whole, and may appear in two places at once.

Like humans, the Tuatha Dé Danann are individuals, with their own personalities. They are not perfect and can make mistakes, but are so much wiser and older than human beings that they make mistakes but rarely. They have friends, enemies, and emotions.

Those emotions, however, are subtly different from those of humans, as are many other of their characteristics. The Tuatha Dé Danann do not have needs corresponding to hunger, thirst, exhaustion, or any similar limitations. I am not aware that they ever sleep or feel physical pain. Their makeup being non-physical, they do not have glands or brains, which means that thoughts and emotions alike are processed in ways completely alien to the usual methods of humans. Their sense of space is different from ours, as are their senses in general. They are aware of much more than human beings, have senses and modes of perception we can only guess at. They appear to have something analogous to sexual reproduction, but the particulars must be very different. For some reason, they are often very curious about human reproduction, and delight in sexual and romantic relations with humans. In addition, they are mostly very old. Even the very youngest we are likely to encounter will have lived centuries, and the greater Gods and Goddesses are literally billions of years old. All this makes the Tuatha Dé Danann inherently mysterious to the human understanding. We find them hard to comprehend. Their motives and actions will always have a strange quality, and there will always be things we miss. They, too, have some trouble understanding and sympathizing with human motivations, but they are infinitely more experienced in this area than we.

Despite the differences between the two races, the Tuatha Dé Danann are overall well-disposed to the human race. They seem to like us, to be willing to accept our worship, to answer our prayers, and in general to get along. It may well be that they see something of their ancient past in us, but it is impossible to be sure. Conversely, we may be attractive to them as a result of our sheer differences, or perhaps we are a project or charge of theirs. Still, they are powerful, and can become angry, particularly with dishonorable behavior or disrespect. It is a mistake to assume that they can be trifled with or treated badly, or that their patience is limitless.

Although they appear to be a sort of non-human race, it would be a mistake to regard them as "extraterrestrials". They have, as far as I know, inhabited this world since it was formed. Most of its natural processes and features, from storms to forests, to oceans, to a moon at the right distance to most benefit life, to the make-up of the rest of the solar system, are the result of their intervention. In short, the terrestrial world reflects, in an imperfect, as yet half-formed way, their own nature. If we are to regard ourselves as native to the Earth (and what else can we be?), I think it would be a serious mistake to regard the Earth's creators and shapers, who have been here billions of years longer than we, as "extraterrestrial". They are the true natives of the Earth, and it is we who are the newcomers.

**Divine Names:** Divine names give us many clues about the nature of individual Gods, but fall far short of giving us true or absolute knowledge of them. In simple point of fact, except in a single case, we do not have knowledge of the true names of Irish deities. And in that case, the true name we are given is an unpronounceable jumble of seeming nonsense-words, with no apparent relation to anything in any form of Gaelic, or, indeed, any other language. In short, the Gods preserve their mystery, and their power. Unlike in Ceremonial Magick, where one may command various angels and demons using the power of their names, we simply do not know names of such power from the corpus of myth, and even if we had them, they are clearly too alien for us to speak or understand.

The names we do have are essentially descriptive epithets which tell us something, but not everything, about the beings they name. The name Lugh, for example, clearly comes from an Old Celtic root meaning something like "Light", or perhaps "Light Flash". The Dagda's name/title means "The Good God", as we shall see, and this tells us something about him, as well. Most deities have a variety of other names and titles, which also tell us much about them. For example, one of the Dagda's titles is "Tri Carboid Roth", or "Three Chariot Wheels". This provides solid evidence of his connection to the old Gaulish Taranis, whose symbol was the chariot wheel. A few of the deity names we have are of unclear origin or meaning. In most of these cases, however, there are still other names and titles to rely on.

Names, then, provide us clues as to the natures of the Gods, ways of connecting to them. By learning and meditating on the names of the Gods, we may to that extent understand and connect to their inner nature. Luckily, we have a good deal more than names to draw on. We also have a plethora of symbols, animals, weapons, tools, and other sacred associations.

**Divine Symbols, Weapons, Animals, and Iconography:** The greatest source of linkage to the true nature of our Gods comes from a consideration of their symbols. It is really in the realm of symbolism that the most important truths about the divine nature are conveyed. It must be pointed out that a given deity's weapons or treasures are not possessions in the usual human sense. Rather, they are expressions of that God or Goddess's inner essence, less property than a part of the deity, expressing profound truths about him or her. In addition, they often possess properties or even personalities of their own, which illuminate that of their owner. The Spear of Lugh, for example, is much more than a weapon. It is also a sentient being, filled with ferocity, and barely kept in check. It is restless and self-willed. It is a symbol of the lightning bolt, the ray of light, the flash of inspiration, the light of knowledge. It pierces, penetrates, reveals, destroys. It is an extension of the God himself, and tells us much about him. The symbols of a deity are much more conducive to meditation than the name. The symbols speak directly to the unconscious mind, and so can "tune us in", so to speak to the energy, the feel, the essence of a divine being. By meditating on the symbols of the Gods, and how these symbols relate to one another, we can bring our religion into our souls.

## Section 1, Subsection a): The Déithe Adhartha

The term Déithe Adhartha (pronounced jay-huh a-ya-ra-ha) literally translates as "Gods of Worship", and is the standard medieval and modern term for the old Irish Gods and Goddesses[1]. It is really a compound of two words. Déithe is the plural of Dia (juh), the word for "God"[2]. The word for "Goddess" is Bandia (bawn-juh), which literally translates as "woman God"[3]. The modern Irish terms derive from a pair of words in Old Celtic, or Archaic Old Irish: *Dêwos*, meaning God, and *Dêwâ*, meaning Goddess[4]. Note how the word in Old Celtic has a feminine ending. It was not necessary, in those days, to use a term meaning "Woman God"! However, the period when the Old Celtic word endings dropped off Irish words corresponds to the period in which Christianity was introduced. As a result, the word for God was assumed to be masculine, and a new word was needed for female deities from the old pantheon. Hence, *Bandia*.

The old term *Dêwos* actually means something like "Shining One". It is derived from the old Indo-European *Dyeu-*, a name for the shining sky Gods[5]. This tells us a bit about how the earliest Celtic peoples thought about their deities. They thought in terms of light, the sky, and perhaps of the kind of mixed order and mystery which the heavens invoke in most people's eyes. A *Dêwos*, or *Dêwâ*, then, was and is a shining being of light, basically beneficent, connected to the regular cycles of the cosmic order, yet essentially mysterious, powerful, and not more to be trifled with than the heavens.

The Adhartha part of the term comes from the word Adhradh, a word meaning "adoration" or "worship". Oddly, this is a Latin loanword, which entered the Irish language by way of the influence of the Church in the early years of Christianization[6]. For this reason, we cannot regard it as the old, pre-Christian term for the greater deities, but, as we have no other term, and "Déithe Adhartha" has been in use for about fifteen hundred years now, we have little choice but to use it.

So, then, the Déithe Adhartha are the greater Gods and Goddesses, the oldest, most powerful, and most honored among the Tuatha Dé Danann. As we shall see, they tend to be quite varied in their concerns, each having a wide variety of interests and areas of influence. In this, they differ from the Gods of, say, the Greeks, which were each much narrower in focus. Likewise, though they may have various localities which are their favorites, they are not limited by time or space. They can hear and answer prayers from anywhere. They may be the ancestors of particular families, but they take their worshippers from among all people, and are not limited in their sphere of influence to their descendants.

We can learn much more about them by looking at them individually:

1. **Dánu (Daw-nuh)**
   A. Meaning of Name: Not known. May be related to a term meaning "low", or "moist"[7].
   B. Other Names and Epithets: Dánu is also called Anu, whose name is also difficult to translate[8]. Dánu may be identified in later times with St. Ann, or with the Virgin Mary[9]. She is called "Mother of the Irish Gods".
   C. Place in Myth: Dánu is called Danann in the Book of Invasions, and is held to be one of the daughters of Ernmas, or "Iron Death", a figure about whom nothing is known[10]. In the Book of Invasions, she is often identified with the Mórrígan, and called one of the Tri

Mórrígna[11]. In Cormac's Glossary, she is called "Mater Deorum Hibernensis", or "Mother of the Irish Gods"[12]. Other than this, she does not figure prominently in mythology. It should be noted, however, that a number of local Cailleacha, or supernatural crones, are called by names similar to Anu[13].

D. Place in Ideology: Dánu is the Mother of the Gods, the Ancestral Goddess, and the Goddess of wells, wisdom, nurturing, fertility, solitary standing stones, mountains, deer, wolves, wild goats, and wild cattle[14].

E. Place in Ritual: Dánu is good to call on for wisdom, nurturing, fertility, or wealth. It is often good to worship her by a well, a river, or a fertile field, but any location will work except one which is in some way impure (for example a land-fill, a sewer, or someplace where violent crimes have often happened).

F. Symbols, Weapons, and Treasures: None known. In a sense all of the Earth is Dánu's treasure.

G. Sacred Places: The Paps of Anu, two hills in Munster[15].

2. **An Mhórrígan (Uh Wor-ree-yun)**

A. Meaning of Name: Probably, "Great Queen", the translation of "Queen of Phantoms" requires a word for phantom which does not, in fact, exist in any known Celtic language[16]. May also be related to the Munster Goddess Mor Muman; the translation of "Queen Mor" is possible, though unsubstantiated[17].

B. Other Names and Epithets: "Queen of Battles", "the Gray-Haired Mórrígan"[18]. The Mórrígan is also identified with a number of other deities, among them Dánu, Macha, the Badb Catha, and Nemain[19].

C. Place in Myth: The Mórrígan was also a daughter of Ernmas, and supposedly the wife of Néit, whose name meant "Battle", and who may or may not be identified with Nuada[20]. She met the Dagda at the River Unius and had sex with him, thereafter prophesying victory for the Tuatha Dé Danann over the Fomors[21]. She was sought as an advisor by Lugh before the Second Battle of Mag Tuired, and chanted a war-poem at the beginning of that battle[22]. During the battle, she and the God Ogma killed a mighty Fomor by the name of Indech, and then shared his blood with the Tuatha Dé Danann, that they might gain his strength[23]. After the battle, she prophesied peace and plenty for the Tuatha Dé Danann, though she also predicted a degenerate distant future age, which can probably be identified with the present[24]. During the Táin Bó Cuailgne, the Mórrígan came to Cúchulainn and offered herself to him25. When he refused her, she worked to hinder him, though she allowed him to win great glory before causing his death26.

D. Place in Ideology: The Mórrígan is the Goddess of fate, sex, war, prophecy, and frenzy. In general, Dánu and the Mórrígan may be identified with one another. It can be said that the Mórrígan is the dark aspect of Dánu, or that Dánu is the light aspect of the Mórrígan. The two ideas are in fact the same. In any case, the union of Dánu/the Mórrígan is the Supreme Being of Ancient Irish Religion. The Mórrígan may be identified with the leader of the Wild Hunt, which is the nocturnal procession of souls journeying to the Otherworld. Note that the Wild Hunt rides only in winter.

E. Place in Ritual: The Mórrígan should be called on with some caution, but may, indeed be called on. It is most important to be wholly clear about one's intentions, and completely sincere. She may be called on for divination, wisdom, victory, protection, and, paradoxically, to make peace. She is particularly the patron of warriors, and also of women.

F. Symbols, Weapons, and Treasures: The main symbol of the Mórrígan is the raven27. Three ravens seen together usually announce her presence, and, in some stories, may foretell the fates of those who encounter them28. She is said to have a chariot pulled by a very odd horse, and two good javelins29. In some stories, she has a red cow, while in others she takes the form of a red cow30. She may take many forms, among them raven, cow, wolf, eel, young woman, and old woman. Her clothing is usually rich. Often, the color red is associated with her31.

G. Sacred Places: There is a district in modern County Louth known as Gort na Mórrígna, or, the Mórrígan's Field. Fulacht na Mórrígna, in County Tipperary is an ancient "cooking spot" known as the Mórrígan's Hearth. Mur na Mórrígna, or Mound of the Mórrígan is found in the Boyne Valley. Tireeworigan, in County Armagh is derived from the name meaning "Land of the Mórrígan". The place where the Mórrígan met the Dagda on the river Unius, in County Donegal, is sacred to them both, and is called the "Bed of the Couple"32.

3. **An Badb Catha (uh bav caa)**
   A. Meaning of Name: Battle Crow.
   B. Other Names and Epithets: None known, but strongly identified with the Mórrígan. The Badb Catha, often just called the Badb,

is one of the Tri Mórrígna, or "Three Mórrígans" along with, variously, the Mórrígan, Dánu, Nemain, and Macha[33]. She may, or may not, be identified with the mysterious Scáthach, who trained Cúchulainn.

    C. Place in Myth: Often the name of the Badb is used interchangeably in myth with the Mórrígan[34]. She is known for an appearance at the Battle of Clontarf in 1014 AD, in which she danced above the points of the spears of the warriors[35].

    D. Place in Ideology: The Badb is that aspect of the Mórrígan who rejoices most in the slaughter of war. She stirs up conflict that it may be won by the good and the right.

    E. Place in Ritual: The Badb Catha may be called on for victory in war and fighting, or for excellent combat skills.

    F. Symbols, Weapons, and Treasures: Crows and ravens, particularly the hooded crow, a type of crow native to the British Isles. Like the Mórrígan, she may appear as a crow, a young woman, or an old woman.

    G. Sacred Places: None known.

**4. Nemain (Nevoin or Newhoin)**

    A. Meaning of Name: From a Gaulish name meaning either "She of the Sacred Grove", or "Great Sacred"[36]. Has come to mean "terror" or "awe", but this is a later development.

    B. Other Names and Epithets: Nemain is one of the Tri Mórrígna, and, as such, strongly identified with the Mórrígan[37]. One of the most famous, and most feared, of the forms of Nemain is the Bean Nighe, or Washer at the Ford, who appears to warriors in the form of a woman washing blood from their clothing. The Bean Nighe is an omen of death[38].

    C. Place in Myth: She makes only a few appearances in myth. In one of these, she sends fear and nightmares onto the men of Ireland when they march on Ulster[39].

    D. Place in Ideology: Nemain is that aspect of the Mórrígan who brings terror, nightmares, and defeat, usually to enemies of the Gods.

    E. Place in Ritual: Not recommended, though it may be possible that Nemain, as the Goddess of Terror, might also be able to cure terror, or protect one from fear.

    F. Symbols, Weapons, and Treasures: None known.

    G. Sacred Places: None known.

## 5. Macha (Macha or Whacha, with the ch like in German loch)

A. Meaning of Name: Not known. May in some way be related to the word Ech, meaning "horse".

B. Other Names and Epithets: Many. Most of the local territorial Goddesses of Ireland are in some sense aspects of her. She is called Macha Mong Rua, "Macha of the Red Tresses", an apparent reference to her having red hair[40]. The heads taken in battle are referred to as "Macha's Mast" or "Macha's Acorn Crop"[41]. She is one of the Tri Mórrígna, and so has a strong identification with the Mórrígan[42].

C. Place in Myth: There are very many Macha myths, which to some extent contradict each other. She is known as the wife of Neimheadh ("sacred"), the first divine being to settle in Ireland, according to some accounts in the Book of Invasions[43]. As such, she would have an ancestral role similar to Dánu. In another myth, she is the daughter of the old Irish king Áedh Rua, who shared the kingship with his two brothers. When Áedh Rua died by accidental drowning, this version of Macha defeated her uncles to become ruler of Ireland[44]. The best known incarnation of Macha, however, is the wife of Chrundchu mac Agnomain, an Ulster landowner. Chrundchu was a widower, and Macha came to him one day, and began to live as his wife. They got on well. One day, Chrundchu went to the court of Conchobar, king of Ulster, and there boasted that his wife could outrun horses. Conchobar called for her to be brought to the court to prove this assertion. She was heavy with child at this time, in the last stage of pregnancy. She asked to be allowed to return home, but Conchobar insisted that she race his horses to prove what her husband had said, on pain of her husband being killed if she refused. She called three times to the crowd of people to relent, each time in the name of the mothers who bore them. The crowd also refused. So, she raced Conchobar's horses and won, then died or disappeared at the end of the track, after giving birth to twins, some say twin foals. As she lay at the end of the track, she cursed the men of Ulster that they would suffer nine days the pangs of labor in the time of their greatest need. Emain Macha, the capital of ancient Ulster is named "The Twins of Macha", from this event[45].

D. Place in Ideology: Macha is the Goddess of sovereignty, motherhood, the Earth, and horses. It is Macha who is that aspect of Dánu/the Mórrígan who gives legitimate power to kings and rulers.

E. Place in Ritual: Macha may be called on by rulers, by mothers, and by children. She will advise rulers as to the proper way, and she will always protect the family. She may also be called on by those who work with the Earth or with livestock, especially horses.

F. Symbols, Weapons, and Treasures: Macha's symbol above all is the horse, often seen as a pair of horses, or as a gray or white mare[46]. She usually takes the form of a young, red-headed woman of matronly aspect.

G. Sacred Places: Emain Macha (modern Navan Fort), the ancient capital of Ulster is the place most sacred to her[47]. Armagh, derived from Ard Macha, or the "Hill of Macha", is also very sacred to her[48]. She is depicted on Corleck Hill, County Cavan, as a white horse, as she also is on a site in Britain[49].

## 6. Lugh (Loo)

A. Meaning of Name: "Light", or possibly "Lightning"[50]. A few scholars have suggested alternate etymologies based on words like "oath", but none of these have met with general acceptance[51].

B. Other Names and Epithets: Lugh is called mac Ethlinn, or Son of Eithne. He is also called Lamhfhada, or "Long Hand", and Samildánach, or "Master of All the Arts"[52]. In later times, Lugh can be identified with both St. Michael, and St. Molua, whose name may mean "My Lugh", or perhaps "Servant of Lugh."[53]

C. Place in Myth: Lugh is the son of Cian, one of the Tuatha Dé Danann, and Eithne, the daughter of Balor, a king of the Fomors. Now, Balor had heard a prophecy that his son would cause his death, so he locked his daughter in a tower, and would let no one see her. Cian, however got in with the use of magic, and fell in love with Eithne. The two escaped, pursued by Balor and the Fomors, until they came among the Tuatha Dé . Here, Eithne gave birth to the infant Lugh. Lugh was fostered in the Otherworld, in order to keep him safe from the Fomors[54]. Some say that his foster father was Manannán[55], other accounts say Goibhniu[56], and still others name one Eochaidh Garb mac Duach, an Otherworld king never mentioned anywhere else[57]. In any case, in his fosterage, Lugh soon grew to master all of the arts known to the Gods, and eventually surpassed even his Teachers. When he came at last to the court of the Tuatha Dé Danann as a young man, he was admitted as the "Master of All the Arts", once he had demonstrated his many skills[58]. Nuada, seeing his skill, appointed him to lead the war against the Fomors, and so he planned what would be the Second Battle of Mag Tuired[59]. During the battle, he killed Balor with a sling, or, in some versions of the tale, with his spear. In any case, the death of Balor meant the collapse of the Fomorian line, and the victory of the Gods[60]. In the years after the Battle, Lugh appeared to many kings and rulers, and also was the father of the hero Cúchulainn[61].

D. Place in Ideology: Lugh is the God of Lightning, which is symbolized by his spear[62]. He is the divine patron of kings and rulers[63]. He is a patron also of sorcerers and druids, as well as of all artisans. He is the God of Light. He can be a trickster, at times, but is normally straightforward. The esoteric significance of the Second Battle of Mag Tuired refers to the winning of the harvest in the autumn, with the coming of storms right around his feast at Lughnasadh. In this sense, Lugh is also a God of the Harvest[64].

E. Place in Ritual: Lugh can be called on for almost everything. He is particularly known for the giving of wisdom, assistance with arts and crafts, and victory. He can at times, however, be a demanding deity, who wishes absolute devotion from those attached to him.

F. Symbols, Weapons, and Treasures: Lugh's symbol is above all the spear, which represents the flash of lightning, and also the light of wisdom[65]. He also has a sword, a pair of javelins, and a dog which turns water to mead[66]. One of Lugh's treasured weapons is the Tathlum, a sling bullet made from the brains of enemy hardened in lime, which cannot be resisted[67]. Lugh's animals include the raven, the wren, the lynx, and the wolf[68].

G. Sacred Places: Loch Lughborta, near Uisneach, is sacred to Lugh, as are many other mounds, and places in Ireland. There are literally dozens of other tribes and settlements throughout the Celtic world which are named for him, and therefore sacred to him[69].

7. **Nuada (Noo-uh-duh)**
   A. Meaning of Name: Not known. A few scholars have suggested possible connections to words meaning "cloud" or "mist", but this is very far from being substantiated[70].
   B. Other Names and Epithets: Nuada is called Airgetlám after his silver hand or arm[71].
   C. Place in Myth: Nuada is the King of the Tuatha Dé Danann at the time that they enter the world. In the 1st Battle of Mag Tuired, against the Fir Bolg, he is wounded in battle, and loses his arm. Because a "blemished" man cannot be king, he must give up his throne. The Dian Cécht, the physician to the Gods, fashions him a new arm made of silver, which is so cunningly made that it duplicates the original in every way. Nuada was followed on the throne by Bres the Fomor, son of the Fomor Elatha, and Banba of the Tuatha Dé

Danann. While Bres is king, the Dian Cécht attempts to figure out a way to restore Nuada's original arm. Shortly after Bres is deposed as king, he succeeds in this, and Nuada's original arm is restored to him. Now "unblemished", Nuada is able to take his throne again. He gives it up temporarily to Lugh, who leads the war against the Fomors, but then returns to the throne after the war[72].

D. Place in Ideology: Nuada in Irish Tradition is a figure midway between his Gaulish War-God antecedent, and the Arthurian concept of the Wounded King. He is the Sky God, the God of the Sword, the God of Warriors and the Protector of Boundaries[73]. Yet, he is also the God of self-sacrifice, who gives up his throne for his people.

E. Place in Ritual: Nuada may be called on for healing, interestingly enough, and for the strength to give of oneself. He may be called on for victory, and for aid in war. He still has enough of the old Gaulish and Indo-European concept in him that one may also call on him for justice, and to safeguard oaths.

F. Symbols, Weapons, and Treasures: Nuada's greatest treasure and symbol is his sword, which cannot be resisted[74]. He also has the silver hand, of course.

G. Sacred Places: Nuada has a number of temples throughout Europe under his Gaulish names. In one sense, any fenced or set-aside land is sacred to him[75]. Even more than sacred places, Nuada is known for his connections to a number of famous Irish tribes. The tribes/dynasties of the Eoganachta, Dál Riada, Ulaid, Laigin, and Osraighe are descended from him. The Dál Riada are particularly important, for this means that all Scots Highlanders can in some sense be regarded as his descendánts[76].

## 8. An Dagda (uh Daw-juh)

A. Meaning of Name: "Good God", not in sense of morally good, but in the sense of "good at everything"[77]. I should point out that, though his name does not have moral connotations, the Dagda was no slouch in the moral sphere, either. While there are tales showing him in a humorous light, there are none showing him as dishonorable.

B. Other Names and Epithets: Many. The Dagda is actually a title or nickname. His personal name is Eochaidh, which is connected to the word for "horse". He is called Ollathair, or "Allfather", Áedh, or "Flame", and Rua Rofhessa, or "Red One of Great Knowledge"[78]. He is sometimes called An Dagda Mór, or "The Great Dagda". He has at least a dozen more names, with various meanings that connect him to a variety of earlier Gaulish divinities, and also to diverse types of fertility symbolism.

C. Place in Myth: The Dagda came with the Tuatha Dé Danann, and fought in the 1ˢᵗ Battle of Mag Tuired. He was much oppressed by Bres, being made to carry firewood and build forts, all on very short rations. After the expulsion of Bres, and the coming of Lugh, the Dagda accompanied Lugh to seek the help of the Mórrígan against the Fomors. He met the Mórrígan at the River Unius, in Donegal, and had sex with her, after which she prophesied victory for the Tuatha Dé Danann. He traveled about the countryside before the 2ⁿᵈ Battle of Mag Tuired, spying out the Fomorian host. While on this journey, he met the daughter of Indech, and persuaded her to join the side of the Tuatha Dé Danann. He also served as an ambassador or messenger to the Fomors on at least one occasion during the long lead-up to the battle. He fought in the battle, killed many Fomors, and was among those to capture Bres[79]. After the war against the Fomors there are still many stories of him

D. Place in Ideology: The Dagda is the God of thunder, rain, fire, fertility, generosity, and prosperity. He is the most giving of the Gods, a model of maleness based on the ability to provide and protect, rather than on dominance or conflict. Like the Germanic Thunor, whom he closely resembles, the Dagda is the divine patron of the common people, and not of kings or lords. He is also a God of wisdom, but his wisdom is the mystical "Great Knowledge" of spiritual truth, rather than the many diverse arts of Lugh.

E. Place in Ritual: The Dagda is good to call on for prosperity above all else. In addition, he may be called on for fertility of humans or animals, for protection, for spiritual wisdom, for good weather, for protection against fire, or for protection against oppression.

F. Symbols, Weapons, and Treasures: The Dagda's symbol is the Cauldron, which feeds all who come to it[80]. His weapon is the club or hammer.[81] He also has a harp which was briefly captured by the Fomors during the 2ⁿᵈ Battle of Mag Tuired. However, when the Dagda came close to it, it leaped off the wall on which the Fomors had kept it, and killed several of them itself[82]. The Horse, specifically the stallion, is sacred to the Dagda, as is the oak tree.

G. Sacred Places: The "Bed of the Couple", in County Donegal, on the River Unius, is sacred to both the Dagda and the Mórrígan[83]. The Grianán Ailigh, in Donegal may once have been sacred to him, though it is no longer regarded as so today[84]. The Brugh na Boine, currently known as Newgrange Tumulus, is sacred to the Dagda, though it is currently inhabited by his son Angus mac Óg[85].

## 9. Brigid (Bree-yij)

A. Meaning of Name: According to most scholars, the name Brigid comes from a British form of a Gaulish name meaning "High One"[86].

B. Other Names and Epithets: Very many. Typical epithets include "Most Excellent Goddess", "Shield Woman", "Companion Woman", "Mother Brigid", and many others[87]. In addition, she has survived the coming of Christianity as St. Brigid, who in Irish and Scottish Catholic folklore is known as the midwife of Christ, and has been one of the most popular of saints for over one thousand years[88].

C. Place in Myth: Oddly, for so prominent a Goddess, Brigid has little role in myth. She is known as the daughter of the Dagda, and in a few traditions as the wife of Bres[89]. She eventually married Tuireann, or else Tuireann is another name for Bres, and bore the Three Sons of Tuireann – Brian, Iuchar, and Iucharba, who became enemies of Lugh, in some myths killing his father[90].

D. Place in Ideology: Brigid is the Goddess of fire, which is called the "Fiery Dart of Brigid"[91]. Her association with fire leads her to become the Goddess of the Hearth, and one of several divine protectors of the family[92]. In addition, it gives rise to her best known role, the "Lady of Poetry, Smithcraft, and Healing"[93]. She is also a Goddess of protection and, particularly, purification, as befits a Goddess of fire and light.

E. Place in Ritual: Brigid may be called on for protection, particularly of the home or family, for purification, exorcism, or for assistance in any of her patron arts. In addition, she may be called on to protect from fire. Her great and famous compassion allows her to be called on, particularly by women, for almost any purpose.

F. Symbols, Weapons, and Treasures: The most important symbol of Brigid is Brigid's Wheel, a three or four armed figure made from straw. The four armed version of Brigid's Wheel is also known as Brigid's Cross, though it is really a different design from the Christian Cross[94]. The flame is also a symbol of Brigid.

G. Sacred Places: The now ruined Abbey of Kildare was built on a shrine to Brigid, and became a "Christian" "abbey" where an eternal flame was kept by nuns who wore a special dress of red and white[95]. It is easily the most sacred of the countless Brigid-shrines scattered throughout Ireland. In addition, Drumeague, County Cavan, is a mountain and community sacred to her96.

10. **Áine (Awn-yuh)**
   A. Meaning of Name: Not known. It may be connected to words meaning "heat", "brightness", or "speed"97. It may also be related to the name Anu, or, then again, it may not.
   B. Other Names and Epithets: Áine is also called Grian, which means "Sun", as well as "Queen of the Fairies of South Munster"98.
   C. Place in Myth: Áine is only rarely mentioned in myth. She is listed as the wife or daughter of Manannán, depending on the source99. She features in a number of stories in various parts of Ireland which involve her affairs with, or, unfortunately, rapes by chieftains100.
   D. Place in Ideology: Áine is the Sun-Goddess, the Lady of Blossom, and the Goddess of Love, as shown by her numerous mortal lovers107. She is the Protector of Crops, particularly in summertime, when her festival is held101.
   E. Place in Ritual: Áine may be called on to bless crops or gardens. She may be called on in affairs of the heart. The light of the sun is known for its protective properties and its power to purify. For this reason it may be possible to call on Áine for these purposes.
   F. Symbols, Weapons, and Treasures: None known beyond the sun itself.
   G. Sacred Places: There are a number of places sacred to Áine. The hill of Cnoc Áine, in County Limerick is sacred to her, and was a site of rituals dedicated to her into recent times. There is another Cnoc Áine in County Derry, which has next to it a well called Tobar Áine. The wild glen of Alt na Síon, also in County Derry, near Cnoc Áine, and the adjacent fort called Lios Áine are both sacred to her. Knockmany Hill, in County Tyrone is also named for, and sacred to, Áine. Áine is an ancestor of the family O'Corra, and is said to wail in Alt na Síon when an O'Corra dies. In addition, Áine is said to be ancestral to the Eóghanachta, the royal dynasty of ancient Munster102.

11. **Manannán mac Lir (Mananan mucklur)**
   A. Meaning of Name: Not known. Clearly Manannán's name is related to that of the Isle of Man in some manner, and the patronymic mac Lir indicates that he is the son of the sea God Ler. Beyond that, however, little is sure.

B. Other Names and Epithets: Manannán is called "Son of the Wave", and "God of Headlands. He may be the same as the Otherworld ferryman Barinthus, whose name means "White Beard", in Latinized Irish[103].

C. Place in Myth: Manannán is known more for appearing in myths than for myths that center around him. He is one of the three Gods listed as the foster father of Lugh. He is possibly the father or husband of Áine[104]. His wife is also called Fand[105], which may mean that Áine is in fact Manannán's daughter, or that Fand is merely Áine by another name. Fand is famous for her brief affair with the hero Cúchulainn[106]. Manannán also appears in several of the tales called Imrama, or "Voyages", meaning voyages to the Otherworld. Usually he helps the heroes of these tales during a storm at sea. In one of these stories we learn that to Manannán the sea appears to be a plain covered with purple flowers, and that therefore he can ride his chariot across it[107]. Manannán is also famous for appearing to many people in real history. The most famous of these is his appearance in various forms, both human and not, at a feast put on at Ballyshannon, east of Donegal Bay, by Black Hugh O'Donnell, who died in 1537[108]. In addition, he has continued to be sighted by people in the Scottish Highlands down to the present day.

D. Place in Ideology: Manannán is most of all the Opener of the Way, the traveling deity who is invoked to guide prayer and invocations to the other Gods[109]. In addition, he is the divine patron of ships, of sailors, of merchants, and of all who travel for a living[110]. Manannán is also the guide to the Otherworld, at least of living visitors, and perhaps of at least some of the dead, as well.

E. Place in Ritual: Manannán can be called on in any ritual, to open the way to the Otherworld, and to aid in reaching the other Gods[111]. In his own right, he may be called on for help in any business affairs, in sales, in traveling, in sailing, and in storms at sea. Manannán may also be called on for wisdom, whether the wisdom of the Otherworld, or the wisdom learned by one who travels in this world.

F. Symbols, Weapons, and Treasures: Manannán's symbol is a special form of triskellion, with feet at the bottom of the three legs, enclosed in a circle[112]. He also is known for having more treasures than any other deity. The Corr Bolg, or Crane Bag is his famous bag, a small bag on the outside, but on the inside big enough to hold all of Manannán's wealth[113]. His boat shines like the sun and is called Wave Sweeper. He also has the sword called "the Answerer", two javelins or spears, and the chariot in which he rides on the sea[114].

Pigs, dogs, and birds are sacred to him. His pigs are famous for regenerating after being eaten. Some identify them as the pigs eaten at the Feast of Age, which bestow immortality.

G. Sacred Places: The entire Isle of Man is sacred to Manannán, as are the Manx as a people. There are also numerous points of land in the Scottish Highlands which, according to local tradition, are sacred to Manannán, and where he was worshipped into the 18th and 19th centuries. Manannán also has an entire world dedicated to him, the hidden Otherworld called Emain Ablach, or the Isle of Apples, which is another form of the Celtic Otherworld as a whole, and may or may not be the land of the dead[115].

## 12. Angus mac Óg (Awng-gus mock Oag)

A. Meaning of Name: Angus is probably derived from the Old Celtic Oinogustus, meaning "One Choice"[116]. The meaning of such a name remains unknown. Mac Óg, however is a title meaning either "Son of Young" or "Young Son", and is therefore not a patronymic. It is this part of the name which connects the Irish Angus to his Continental equivalents[117].

B. Other Names and Epithets: None known, though Angus is spelled a rather large number of ways, among them Oengus, Aengus, and Oenghus. He is regarded as the son of the Dagda and Boann[118].

C. Place in Myth: Angus is best known for the story "The Dream of Angus", in which he has a dream of a beautiful woman night after night. He falls in love with her, and soon is sick with wanting her. Eventually, it is revealed to him that she really exists; her name is Cáer Ibormeith (Yew Berry), and he can find her at Loch Bel Dracon, in County Tipperary. Cáer goes there every Samhain with 150 other maidens, all in swan form. Angus goes to the lake, and finds her. The two of them then return to the Brugh na Boine in swan form[119]. Angus is also known for assisting various famous pairs of lovers, among them the famous Diarmuid and Gráinne[120].

D. Place in Ideology: Angus is the divine patron of youth, summer, love, and joy. He is also a powerful magician, famed for invisibility and illusions. As the bringer of summer, Angus may be celebrated at either the vernal equinox, or at Beltaine.

E. Place in Ritual: Angus may be called on by lovers, or by magicians seeking to learn the art of illusion. He can also be called on the bring cheer, and in hopes of good weather.

F. Symbols, Weapons, and Treasures: Angus has the cloak of invisibility. He also has three birds which sing sweetly, banishing all depression and care[121].

G. Sacred Places: The Brugh na Boine is the place most sacred to Angus. It was originally his father's dwelling, but Angus came to him wishing to borrow it. "For how long do you want it?" asked the Dagda. "For day and night", replied Angus. So, this seeming reasonable, the Dagda lent Angus his house. When he came the next day to reclaim it, Angus wouldn't leave. "But you're time is up", the Dagda protested. "Ah", said Angus, "it is not indeed. You promised me the Brugh for day and night, and it is of day and night that the world is made." And so he kept the Brugh for all time[122]. This story depends on the lack of an indefinite article in Irish; "day and night", and "a day and a night" are exactly the same words in the Irish language. The story also illustrates something about the ancient Irish concept of time – it is made of day and night, of the cyclic alternation of spiritual principles.

## 13.  Boann (Bo-ahn)

A. Meaning of Name: The name Boann means "Great Cow", or may be derived from Bo Finn, meaning "White Cow".

B. Other Names and Epithets: None known. Note that Boann is very rarely called one of the Tri Mórrígna[123], though I personally believe this to be a late and mistaken identification. Note also that her name is sometimes spelled Boand.

C. Place in Myth: Boann is known for having mated with the Dagda in the Brugh na Boine. She manipulated time, so that the two were able to live together for nine months, until the birth of Angus, and yet only one night passed to the rest of the world[124]. She is also known for having gone to the Well of Wisdom for a drink of water. The well burst from its containment and pursued her, until it reached the sea, and became the Boyne River[125]. Boann is usually identified as the Goddess of the Boyne.

D. Place in Ideology: Boann may seem a simple fertility Goddess, but that is rather far from the truth. The truth of her nature is revealed in a bit of rather obscure Irish folklore. According to Daragh Smyth, the moon was called a cow in Irish folk-speech, with the phases identified as follows: the waxing moon as Bó Finn (white cow), the full moon as Bó Rua (red cow), the waning moon as Bó Donn (brown cow), and the dark moon Bó Orainn (dark cow). From this we can see that Boann is actually the moon-Goddess[126]. From the other stories about her, we can see that she is to be identified with the tides, with the sea, and with fertility. Even more, however, we see from the story of her assignation with the Dagda that she was the Goddess of Time. This, of course, fits with the lunar calendar of the ancient Gaels, which must therefore be under the patronage of Boann.

E. Place in Ritual: Boann can be called on for fertility, for wealth, for love, and perhaps for guidance. More interestingly, she can in fact be called on to manipulate time to some degree. I myself have experienced this. After I gave a lecture which spoke about Boann, my significant other at that time, Carole, and I drove the entire distance to her home (then in Sturgeon Lake, MN) in about half the time it should have taken us. We had no reason to get home in a hurry. It was almost as if she were merely revealing to us her existence and power.

F. Symbols, Weapons, and Treasures: The moon. The cow is of course Boann's animal.

G. Sacred Places: The Boyne River is sacred to Boann. The Boyne is indeed the most sacred river in Ireland, the Irish Ganges. In Ancient Irish astronomy, the Milky Way was known as the Way of the White Cow, suggesting both a connection between Boann and the Milky Way, and also that the Boyne is in fact the River of Heaven (ie. The Milky Way) reflected on the Earth. The Brugh na Boinne has some connection with Boann, and there are a number of wells sacred to her throughout Ireland.

## 14. Ogma (Oh-muh)

A. Meaning of Name: Not known. Probably the name Ogma is related to the Gaulish Ogmios[127].

B. Other Names and Epithets: Ogma was called the son of Elatha, which would make him at least half-brother to both the Dagda and Bres[128]. He was also called Grianenech (Sunny Face) and Cermait (Honey Tongue)[129].

C. Place in Myth: Ogma was the champion of the Tuatha Dé Danann, and also the most eloquent of them. He and the Mórrígan killed the Fomor Indech during the 2nd Battle of Mag Tuired. Ogma then joined the Dagda and Lugh in a search for the Dagda's harp, which had somehow been captured by the Fomors. The harp was recovered, and then Ogma took part in the capture of Bres. Ogma's sons included Tuireann, and also Cairpre, the Bard of the Tuatha Dé Danann[130].

D. Place in Ideology: From his iconography, we can see that Ogma is a sun-God, and by extension a God of fire[131], as well as a God who combines strength with eloquence. He is the patron of specifically verbal ability, and combines the role of poet with that of warrior[132]. This, of course, springs from his fiery nature, which is at home with the burning heat of violence and also the fire of inspiration.

E. Place in Ritual: Ogma may be called on for protection, especially against fire. More likely, though, he will be called on for strength, martial skills, or poetic inspiration. Like Angus, he may be called on to impart good cheer and lift depression.

F. Symbols, Weapons, and Treasures: Ogma's symbol is a sort of sun-face design. He has a sword which is able to relate all of the events of the 2$^{nd}$ Battle of Mag Tuired from beginning to end. I would guess that it can tell many another story besides[133].

G. Sacred Places: Síd Airceltrai is sacred to Ogma[134].

## Section 1, Subsection c): Na Déithe Danann

The term Déithe Danann means literally "Gods of Art", and refers to the divine patrons of every craft. I have derived it from the traditional term "Tri De Danann" given variously to Brian, Iuchar, and Iucharba, and also to a trio composed variously of Goibhniu, the Dian Cécht and a number of other deities. Déithe Danann in the sense I mean differ from the Déithe Adhartha in being narrower in focus. Where Lugh may be called on as a patron of arts, kings, and also the harvest, or where the Dagda may be called on a God of mystic knowledge, fertility, and protection, the Déithe Danann may only be called upon in the area of their particular arts. In addition, they are considered to serve the Gods with their arts, with Goibhniu being the Smith to the Gods, Dian Cécht being the Physician to the Gods, and so on. Those who practice a given art or craft would do well to pray to the Dia Danann of their particular craft. In Christian times, these deities were often identified with or replaced by the patron saints of the various arts. Traditional prayers to these saints survive to this day.

We will examine only two of the Déithe Danann in detail, to see how they worked in general. A few examples of Déithe Danann for various arts, crafts, and professions are included below:

| Name | Art |
|---|---|
| Goibhniu | Smith |
| Dian Cécht | Physician |
| Credne | Bronzeworker |
| Cairbre | Bard/Poet |
| Mathgan | Sorcerer |
| Figol | Druid |
| Luchta | Wright and Carpenter |

**1. Goibhniu (Guv-nuh)**

A. Meaning of Name: "Smith", or, actually "Smiths"[135].

B. Other Names and Epithets: He is also called in later folklore the Goban Saor, (Go-baun Syur) which means "Builder Goban". He is one of the four sons of Esarg, son of Néit. Of Esarg, nothing else is known. The other three sons of Esarg were the Dian Cécht, Credne, and Luchta[136].

C. Place in Myth: Goibhniu is the smith of the Gods, and so was responsible for making all of their tools, weapons, and metal goods. In addition, he made a number of wonderful devices, or which the most famous are Nuada's silver hand, and, in some tellings, the pigs eaten at the Feast of Age, which kept the Gods immortal. Goibhniu is not only famous for smithcraft, but also as a builder, a brewer, a chef, and as a doting father[137]. In later folklore, the son and daughter of "The Goban Saor" are the heroes of a cycle of amusing and adventurous folktales[138].

D. Place in Ideology: Goibhniu is not all that difficult to understand. He is the God of smithcraft and of artisanship generally. As such, he is the divine patron of all who work with tools or their hands to make things.

E. Place in Ritual: Goibhniu is best to call on when doing smithcraft or other types of craft-work. He can also be called on to aid with all types of machinery, even down to computers. Interestingly, he is also called on in traditional healing-charms, most famously, in one against the prick of a thorn.

F. Symbols, Weapons, and Treasures: In most of the Celtic world, the local equivalent of Goibhniu was pictured with a smith's hammer, tongs, and leather apron, and it certainly seems sensible that these should be the symbols of Goibhniu also. In addition, Goibhniu is, along with Manannán said to own the pigs of the Feast of Age. The healing-charm which invokes him mentions his sharp awl, a tool of either a smith or leather-worker[139].

G.  Sacred Places: Cerdcha Gaibhnenn (Goibhniu's Forge) is a sacred site located in the forest of Glenn Treicim, in the northern part of County Wicklow. The nearby hill of Mullagh Mast is also sacred to Goibhniu. In his later aspect, the Goban Saor, he is said to be from Turvey Strand, probably the modern Fairview Strand, Dublin[140].

2. **The Dian Cécht (John Kecht, with "ch" pronounced like German "loch")**
   A.  Meaning of Name: Oddly, the name appears to mean "God of the Plowshare". Why he is so named is not known.
   B.  Other Names and Epithets: None known.
   C.  Place in Myth: The Dian Cécht is best known as the Physician of the Gods. He was able to bring the warriors killed in the Second Battle of Mag Tuired back to life, provided their brains had not been damaged or their heads cut off. He restored Nuada's original hand, even though much of it had been lost to decay. He is the grandfather of Lugh[141]. He is also known from a rather disturbing story, in which his son, Miach (Mee-uch) developed even better healing skills than his father. The Dian Cécht was filled with jealousy, and struck Miach in the forehead, breaking open his skull. Miach healed this. So, the Dian Cécht struck harder, penetrating to the lining of the brain. Miach healed this also. So, the Dian Cécht struck his son a third time, splitting open the brain. Miach could not heal this, and so he died. The Dian Cécht's daughter, Airmid (Or-midj), buried Miach and spoke certain spells over the grave. As a result, the 365 organs, Múscles and bones of Miach's bodies gave rise to the 365 healing herbs, which grew on his grave and were harvested by Airmid[142].
   D.  Place in Ideology: The Dian Cécht is the physician of the Gods, and so his role is a simple one.
   E.  Place in Ritual: The Dian Cécht may be called on in any endeavor related to healing or medicine, whether one wishes to heal or to be healed.
   F.  Symbols, Weapons, and Treasures: None known.
   G.  Sacred Places: None known.

## Section 1, Subsection b): Éarlaimh

The term Éarlamh (air-lahv) translates as "patron". Depending on whom you ask, it either was first used to refer to the founder of a medieval Christian monastery, who became the patron of the place, and from there came to mean "patron saint"143, or else it is of Pagan date, and originally referred to a patron divinity144. Given that the old Irish certainly had the idea of patron divinities, and there is no other word for them, we have chosen to use the latter interpretation.

An éarlamh, then, is similar to the Déithe Adhartha, but even more narrow in focus than a Dia Danann. Where one of the Déithe Adhartha would be concerned with people, phenomena, and conditions of life without regard to geography, an éarlamh is only concerned with a single region, tribe, family, or major geographical feature. If it happens in, or effects, the éarlamh's area of influence, then it is the éarlamh's concern. If it is not in the Éarlamh's area of influence, then the Éarlamh is not concerned.

Éarlaimh (air-lawv, the plural of éarlamh) can probably be identified with the many local "Kings" and "Queens" of the "Fairies", who are so common in later Irish folklore. Certainly, they rule over the lesser spirit beings in the areas under their rule. As such, and due to their own power in their area of influence, they are worthy of reverence by human beings, whose lives they influence far more than most people would ever imagine.

Note that the category of éarlamh is not exclusive. That is, it is possible for a given deity to be one of the éarlaimh, and also one of the Déithe Adhartha, or a Dia Danann. Lugh, Nuada, and other deities have specific places, tribes, and families to whom they have special relationships, and who are therefore under their protection145. Note also that an éarlamh was often, but not always, an ancestral spirit. This is particularly true of divine patrons of families and tribes. Often, the éarlamh is the first chieftain of the tribe, which is named for him or her.

What follows is a list of examples of éarlaimh from various parts of Ireland, with maybe one or two also important to Scotland. This list is meant as a sample alone, and should not be taken as comprehensive. A complete list of all éarlaimh would be a work unto itself, and, indeed, an ancient example of this exact thing is found in the Dindsenchus.

**Áedh Rua:** Áedh Rua is the spirit of Ess Rua, a waterfall and spring in Ulster. He was the father of one incarnation of Macha, a Milesian king, who peacefully shared the rulership of Ireland with his two brothers for his entire life. He drowned accidentally in the waterfall and so became its spirit. Note that Áedh Rua is not of the Tuatha Dé Danann, but is actually a human spirit[146].

**Almu:** Almu is the spirit of the fortress of Almu, in Leinster. She is also the founder and patron of the family of Muirne of the White Neck, the mother of the hero Finn mac Cumhail. Almu's origin is unclear[147].

**Bui:** Bui is the local deity of the district of Cnogha. She is also the wife of Lugh. Bui is one of the Tuatha Dé Danann [148].

**Carmun:** The patron divinity of the town and fair of Carmun, she was originally a Fomorian queen who was captured during the war against the Fomors and imprisoned there. Eventually, she lost her Fomorian character, being "converted" as it were to the Tuatha Dé Danann, and then becoming the patron of the town where she had been held[149].

**Clíodna:** One of the divine patrons of the province of Munster, Clíodna dwells at Carraig Clíodna, near modern Mallow, in County Cork. She is said to have three sweetly singing birds. On a more sinister note, she is also said to be a banshee who wails to foretell the deaths of the kings of Munster, and to enjoy luring young seamen onto the rocks off Carraig Clíodna in order to take them as her lovers. She is one of the Tuatha Dé Danann, but barely[150].

**Corigend:** The patron spirit of the town of Ailech, the home of the hero Niall Noígiallach, Corigend was imprisoned there by the Dagda for killing one of his sons. He is a harsh and warlike spirit, possibly Fomorian in nature[151].

**Crochen:** Crochen is the patron spirit of the fortress of Cruachan, the capital of ancient Connaught. Originally a handmaiden to Etain, wife of Ogma, she was given the síd of Cruachan in reward for her loyal service. Crochen is one of the Tuatha Dé Danann [152].

**Erne:** Not to be confused with Ériu, Erne is the spirit of Loch Erne, in Connaught. One of the handmaidens of Queen Medb, Erne drowned in the lake. Like Áedh Rua, she is a human spirit[153].

**Fróech:** Fróech is the divine patron of Carn Fróech and Síd Fróech, in Ulster. Originally, he was a warrior, with a human father and a mother of the Tuatha Dé Danann. He was killed by Cúchulainn, and, as he lay dying, he was borne into the síd by a group of women of his mother's people. Fróech is now considered predominantly of the Tuatha Dé Danann [154].

**Nás**: The divine patron of the district of Nás, this Goddess was also a wife of Lugh[155].

**Sinann**: The spirit of the river Shannon, Sinann played a role in a number of early Irish myths, including that of the coming of the Children of Mile[156].

**Téa**: The divine patron of Tara, the seat of the ancient Irish high kings. She was said to dwell at Tara, and was worshipped there. As the patron of the Assembly of Tara, Téa acquired national importance[157].

**Tlachtga**: The divine patron of the town/fortress and Assembly of Tlachtga, it is possible that Tlachtga was once a mortal woman. She is said to have had three babies at once, by three different fathers and to have died of it. She dwells at Tlachtga, and was worshipped there. Like Téa, the importance of the Assembly she patronized gave her fame beyond that of a strictly local deity[158].

**Angus Tuirmech Temrach:** In legend, the High King of Ireland for sixty years, after killing Fergus Fortamail and taking the sovereignty from him. He was known as a good king, who died quietly in bed, and left the rulership of Ireland to one of his sons. He is the ancestor of the *tuatha* of Leath Chuinn and Dal Fiatach[159].

**Áine:** A Bandia Adhartha, Áine is also the divine ancestor of the O'Corras[160].

**Cairbre Cinn Cait:** In English, we would say, Cairbre Cat Head. An aggressive and warlike chieftain, he was the ancestor of the Érainn, along with Áine. He is also associated with the Cloghan Cinn Cait, a landmark in Brandon, County Kerry, also known as the Stepping Stones of Cairbre[161].

**Cairbre Músc:** Cairbre the Elk, the ancestor of the Múscraighe, a branch of the Érainn in County Cork. Cairbre Músc was famed as a poet. The Dál Cairbre also sprang from him[162].

**Laibraid Loingsech:** Leary the Exile, himself a descendant of Nuada, he was the chief ancestor of the Laigin, the royal tribe of Leinster. Laibhraid was forced to leave Ireland for Gaul, when his father was killed. In Gaul, he assembled an army, and returned to Ireland, where he made himself ruler of Leinster in a bloody campaign. He was said to be partially of Fir Bolg descent[163].

**Lugh:** Lugh was possibly the ancestor of the Corco Loigde, as well as of many other tribes[164].

**Manannán mac Lir:** Beside being one of the Déithe Adhartha, Manannán is also the ancestor of the Manx people[165].

**Mog Ruith:** Literally "Slave of the Wheel", Mog Ruith was a famous Druid, about whom clusters a whole cycle of tales, which emphasize his wisdom and skill in magic. He was the ancestor of the Corco Duibhne, who also worshipped the Mórrígan[166].

**Muinremur mac Gerrcind:** One of the heroes of the Red Branch, Muinremur was a warrior of Ulster. He dissected the pig of Mesroida mac Da Tho in the "Story of mac Da Tho's Pig". He was the ancestor of the Mugdornai, a tribe of Ulster[167].

**Niall Noígiallach:** Niall of the Nine Hostages is an historical figure, and a contemporary of St. Patrick. He led his own people out of Connaught on a campaign of conquest in Ulster which broke the power of the Ulaid. In time, he and his sons established themselves as kings of Ireland at Tara, making a unified Ireland possible for the first time. Niall had fourteen sons, most of whom are ancestors of various *tuatha* or at least families. Some of them include:
> **Loegaire:** ancestor of the Kendellans.
> **Conall Crimthainne:** ancestor of the O'Melaghlins.
> **Fiacha:** ancestor of the Mageoghegans and O'Malloys.
> **Maine:** ancestor of the O'Caharny (now Fox), O'Briens, and the Magawleys.
> **Eoghan:** ancestor of the O'Neills proper.

**Conall Gulban:** ancestor of the O'Donnels[168].

**Nuada:** as mentioned in the last lecture, Nuada is the ancestor of the Eóghanachta (through Eóghan Mor), the Dál Riada (through Eochaidh Riada), the Ulaid, the Laigin (through Laibhraidh Loingsech), and the Osraighe[169].

**Sláinge:** A Fir Bolg chieftain, Sláinge is the ancestor of the Gáileoin, a Leinster tribe with connections to the Laigin[170].

## Discovering Éarlaimh

The majority of people reading this book do not live in a currently Celtic country. They are not able to go to the Dindsenchas to learn who the éarlaimh are of the place where they live. What, then, is to be done? How can they establish the important relationship with their local deities? The short answer is: very carefully. The exact technique depends on where one lives, though the methods have a certain family resemblance.

Many people in Europe live in **ex-Celtic** lands. For them, they key is in archaeology. There were in fact local, Celtic deities worshipped all over modern England, France, Belgium, Switzerland, southern Germany northern Spain, northern Italy, Austria, the Czech Republic, and even Slovenia. In these lands, it is as simple as reading up on the archaeology of Iron Age Celtic Europe to figure out who was worshipped where you live, and then resuming the worship of these beings, alongside the better known Déithe Adhartha.

In other parts of the world, including America, it is harder still, but by no means impossible. Almost everyplace on Earth, with the exception of Antarctica, has some sort of native inhabitants, and, including Antarctica, some kind of folklore about it, either of the native peoples or of others. When one looks up native and other folklore, and also place-names, local history, and well-known sacred spots, one rapidly finds certain patterns emerging. Certain spots emerge as holy again and again, held so by culture after culture. Their names often have an eerie similarity. Such similarities are worth looking at, for they tell us something about the place, and the powers who live there.

Such significant or holy places are often of geographical significance. A local river, or the source of a local river, a large mountain that determines much about local weather, a forest which determines the local ecology, a spring in a desert, these are usually the kinds of places which emerge again and again as sacred. The general outline and controlling factors in local landforms are also important. Is your home region dominated by the rivers which cross it? Or by the great and trackless woods? Or by a range of steep hills? Such types of land-forms give clues as to the spiritual powers in any given area.

Finally, a good portion of determining what éarlamh rules any given place must come from the intuition. How does your home region feel to **you**? Chances are, if you sit down, and just let your mind think about it, without trying too hard, you will be able to sense what areas are your own, which ones are your home turf, and where it gives way to another territory. Chances are you already know how your home region **feels** to you, especially if you have traveled, so that you have something to compare it to.

If you explore these feelings, you may learn much. Does your home ground feel like there is a single dominant personality? If so, what is that personality like? Perhaps it feels like there is no single dominant being, but many lesser ones, a tribe of lesser spirits. Such is possible, as we shall see. There are a few areas ruled not by éarlaimh, but by tribes of lesser spirits.

In any case, it is by combining this intuition with such folklore as may exist about your area, and how it was named, and the local geographical features that will lead you, bit by bit, to the local éarlamh. It is not an easy process, but it is indeed possible, and worth doing, for it allows you not only to connect with the realities of the Tuatha Dé Danann, but also with your own land. You can become not only more Gaelic, but also more native to wherever you may live. This is nothing to sneer at.

Once you have some idea of the éarlamh of your place, then the next step is to give him or her a name. Generally, your study will have revealed much about this being, its nature, and perhaps some earlier names. It is now a simple matter of taking those essentials, what makes this being what he or she is, and setting those features into words, and then into Irish or Scots. This is the least difficult part, actually. You will find that a name comes to you pretty rapidly, once you understand how your éarlamh is. It is only necessary also to study the language to translate that name into a Gaelic form.

# Section 2: Na Sinsir

# Characteristics of the Sinsir

B. The Ancestors

Sinsir is a term used to refer to deceased ancestors. It is generally accepted that people live on after death in the Otherworld, and that they are able to affect life in this world. For that reason, and also to remember those we loved when they were alive, the worship of ancestors is an integral part of Irish Pagan tradition. Ancestors accept prayer, offerings, and general praise, though how they will react to these things depends a lot on who they were in life. Generally, personalities do not change much after physical death, or, at least, not right away. People go on holding to the same values they held to for decades when they were alive, changing slowly, as in life, as they learn new things and assimilate new ideas. For the most part, ancestors are not especially powerful, being able to send good and bad fortune, and to give advice, but only on a fairly small scale.

It should be noted, however, that there is no necessary and solid dividing line between Sinsir and other types of spiritual being. Some humans have become éarlaimh, with much greater power that the average ancestor. Also, various éarlaimh, and even Déithe Danann, are seen as the ancestors of certain families even though they have never been human[171].

A summary of the nature and characteristics of the Sinsir is below:

**Terms and Names:** Also called by some Seanathreacha (Old Fathers)[172].

## Bodies and Forms:
1. Immaterial but able to assume appearance or material forms for a short period.
2. Usually take the form they had on life, often when at their physical and mental peak.

## Powers:
1. Able to send good and bad fortune to their descendants.
2. Able to observe without being seen, possibly to read minds and emotions, often, therefore able to impart much information.
3. Of two main types:

a. Those ancestors who have evolved to live without incarnation, who are usually more powerful, and much older.
b. Those who are currently "between lives". These are usually less powerful, and normally incarnate after a period of time, on average ten to twenty years.

## Vulnerabilities:
1. Rowan wood
2. Red Thread
3. Iron/Cold Iron (not effective in my experience)
4. Rites of protection
5. Christian prayers and symbols (ineffective, in my experience, and likely to anger the earliest of them)173

## Motivations/Psychology:
1. Usually concerned with the welfare of their descendants.
2. Often consider themselves to have the right to meddle in the affairs of others, usually "for their own good".
3. Usually continue to have the values, ethics, prejudices, and beliefs they had in life. Those of recent dates are usually still some sort of Christian, though this is very difficult to reconcile with their current environment.
4. Can learn, and so may occasionally change in their beliefs.
May, or may not, respond to prayer.

The greatest and most powerful of the Sinsir is both the ruler of the dead, and a greater deity in his own right. This is Donn, who was the first human being to die in this world, and is therefore the ruler of the human dead. Donn is the ancestor of ancestors, and is, effectively, the ruler of all the others, with the exception of those who have joined the Éarlaimh or Déithe Adhartha. For the most part he takes little interest in the lives of the living, but in all matters involving the human dead, he reigns supreme.

## Donn (Don)
A. Meaning of Name: "Dark", or "Brown", probably meaning something like "Dark One".
B. Other Names and Epithets: Also called Da Derga (Daw Jer-eg-uh), which translates as "Blood-Red God".174
C. Place in Myth: Donn is human in origin, one of the original Sons of Míl. He was the brother of Éremón, the first human kind in Ireland. When the Milesians landed in Ireland, they first met Ériu,

the Goddess of the country. Amairgin the druid promised that the land would be named for her, but Donn disagreed. For this she cursed him that none of his descendants would live in the land. When the Milesian host met Banba, another of the Goddesses of the country, Amairgin made the same promise, and Donn again disagreed. Again he was cursed. When the host met Fótla, the third of the Goddesses of the country, Amairgin again promised to name the land after her, and again Donn refused, and was cursed a third time. When the Milesians met the Gods, they negotiated to set the date of the battle between them. The Gods said that it was not fair that they would not get a chance to keep the Milesians from landing. So, the Milesians returned to their boats, sailed out of sight, and then came to land again. Donn was keeping watch on top of one of the masts. As the boats neared the land, the Gods sent a wind against the human ships. Amairgin used his own magic to quiet the wind, said magic being strengthened by the favor of Ériu, Banba, and Fótla, but not before Donn fell from his mast and died on the deck below. As the first human being to die in Ireland, he became ruler of the Irish dead[175].

D.  Place in Ideology: Donn is at once the ruler of the dead, and the first of the Sinsir. He does not decide when people die, nor is he the guide of their souls, but once they have passed to the Otherworld, he rules them, as long as they are human. In this, he follows an ancient Indo-European pattern[176].

E.  Place in Ritual: Donn would be rare for the living to call upon, as his authority does not extend to this world, though he is commonly invoked by the dead. He might be called on by one wishing to communicate with a particular ancestor, or by one who feels that an ancestor has sent bad fortune unjustly. Donn should also be called on at funerals, and requested to accept the spirit of the departed into his realm.

F.  Symbols, Weapons, and Treasures: None known. There is a remote possibility that the Brown Bull of Cuailgne was associated with him, in which case a brown or black bull might be his symbol or otherwise sacred to him. Note that his colors appear to be black, brown, and blood red[177].

G.  Sacred Places: The Skellig Rocks, off the coast of Munster are sacred to Donn, and are called Teach Duinn (Tech Doon, with the "ch" like in German), meaning "House of Donn". These are held to be a sort of mini-afterworld, where Donn feasted the dead before they went on to the Otherworld proper[178].

## Section 3: Na Daoine Síthe

## Characteristics of the Daoine Síthe

Daoine Síthe is a term I am using as a kind of catch-all for a wide variety of types of nature spirit. Not all of these are to be counted among the Tuatha Dé Danann, though many are among the least of them. Others form independent companies of spirits, neutral in the war between the Gods and their enemies. It is a central part of most forms of Paganism, including Irish, that the natural world is filled with such beings. Humanity is very, very far from alone.

It needs to be stressed that the Daoine Síthe are less like divine beings, and more like a race, or, rather, group of races, with whom humans share their world[179]. They are clearly An-Dhéithe, "not-Gods", and, a such inferior to the Déithe, very much on the same level as humanity. Even those Daoine Síthe among the Tuatha Dé Danann are still as imperfect and variable as ordinary people, and need to be treated with the respect one would give a neighbor or landlord, and not with worship. Offerings to the Daoine Síthe are more on the order of rent payments, or the mutual borrowing that once went on among human neighbors, than like the types of offerings given to the Déithe[180].

Those among the Daoine Síthe who are counted among the Tuatha Dé Danann do give reverence to the Déithe Adhartha, though not in precisely the same way as humans, since they see the Déithe more as ancestors than as deities per se. Those who are not among the Tuatha Dé Danann may in fact be among the Fir Bolg[181], though others are ruggedly independent, acknowledging neither the Gods, nor the Fomors, nor even other similar companies of spirits in some cases.

Note that the line between humans, Daoine Síthe, and Déithe is necessarily vague and blurred. Daoine Síthe can and do ascend to greater power and influence, and the leaders of groups of Daoine Síthe are often éarlaimh. On the other hand, humans can and do join the Daoine Síthe, either before or after death[182]. As the Changeling myth shows, it is even possible for Daoine Síthe to be born into the human world, though this is very rare[183].

A list of their characteristics is below:

## Gods and Spirits 39

**Terms and Names:** Called variously the "Fair Folk", "People of Peace", "Good Folk", "Others", "People of the Mounds", and so on[184].

### Bodies and Forms:
1. Immaterial but able to assume material forms for a short period.
3. Able to take any form consistent with their *Dlúth*.
4. Often appear as normal human beings native to the country they live in[185].

### Powers:
1. Control of fertility and prosperity.
2. Sending of good and bad luck.
3. Able to cause people to become lost and confused.
4. Able to create illusions, most often in old tales, but now and then in reality.
5. Causing and curing of various diseases, especially:
    a. strokes
    b. rheumatism
    c. back pain
    d. paralysis[186]

### Vulnerabilities:
6. Rowan wood
7. Red Thread
8. Iron/Cold Iron (not effective in my experience)
9. Rites of protection
10. Christian prayers and symbols (ineffective, and likely to anger them)[187]

### Motivations/Psychology:
1. Believe themselves to be native inhabitants of the land, and humans to be interlopers.
2. Believe themselves to be entitled to offerings from humans, and to have rights which humans do not.
3. Fiercely protect their privacy, and their property.
4. Have their own code of ethics, which includes:
    a. Keeping their word
    b. Neatness and cleanness
    c. Hospitality
    d. Courtesy and respect
    e. Cheerfulness
    f. Always returning like for like, vengeance, in short

5. Often imitate human customs, games and so on. Occasionally imitate human expectations of their behavior[188].

## Types of Daoine Síthe

This is not a comprehensive list, but merely a setting out of many typical types of Daoine Síthe, both in folklore, and in my experience. I have tried to set out what I believe to be the origin of each type of spirit, and some of its characteristics.

**Black Dogs:** Black Dogs appear in the folklore of every region of the British Isles, and in many other areas besides. They are still seen from time to time, and, as such make their way into many books of "unexplained phenomena". They are usually said to take the form of a very large, shaggy, black animal, usually a canine, with glowing eyes. They range from friendly to dangerous, though most ignore humans or are rather mischievous. They are probably Fir Bolg, though this is very unclear[189].

**Brownie:** The brownie is a popular name for a class of household spirits more accurately called hobs. They are usually attached to a particular house or family, where they perform a variety of cleaning and chores, if given offerings. According to tradition, a neglected brownie may cause all kinds of mischief, or even poltergeist-like phenomena, though this is quite rare. The brownie as such is exceedingly rare in modern times. Other types of household spirit, which send good or bad luck to the household, are far more common. Most such spirits are of Fir Bolg origin, though some are actually ancestral spirits[190].

**Earth Spirits:** There are a wide variety of Earth spirits, inhabiting natural features like soil, rocks, and ordinary hills. They appear in many different forms, but tend to be short and of brownish coloring. They range from the helpful to the dangerous, but most tend to ignore humans unless provoked. Not unnaturally, the welfare of the land is their primary concern. A few are inclined to reward people who care for the land, and to punish those who do not. The majority of Earth Spirits are of Fir Bolg origin[191].

**Merrows:** The Merrows, or Murdhuacha, are a race of sea-spirits known only from Irish and Scottish folklore, and not from the ancient texts. I include them both because of their inherent interest, and because they are one of the best developed races of sea-spirits in Gaelic tradition. They live on the bottom of the sea in societies much like that of human beings, though they are far more skilled in crafts and magic. Surprisingly, they are not water breathers, but can only live underwater with the aid of their red caps and enchanted houses, which supply a breathable atmosphere. Relations between human beings and merrows are basically friendly, with female merrows in particular having a fondness for human men. Still, they were often feared in older times, because their appearance was said to foretell storms. They are of unknown origin[192].

**Merry Dancers:** The Merry Dancers are the old Highland spirits of the aurora borealis. They are said to be divided into two tribes who fight for the affection of the Queen of the Northern Lights. Legend has it that the auroras themselves are the lights of the battle, while the reddish sky which often forms beneath them is the pool of blood it produces. No legend describes any significant interaction between the Merry Dancers and humanity, which is only natural given the different realms the two races inhabit. They also are of unknown origin[193].

**Mine Spirits**: These are the spirits which inhabit mines and shafts, like the Cornish Knockers or the Welsh Coblynau. These spirits are usually very helpful to miners, showing them where to find veins of ore, mostly by means of a knocking sound. They do, however demand small offerings in exchange for their services, and they might withhold their services if the offerings are not forthcoming. They are not usually seen, but are occasionally described as being of horribly ugly appearance, often accompanied by a bluish light. They are probably of mostly Fir Bolg origin[194].

**Seal People:** There are several varieties of seal people in Scottish and Irish folklore. All of them are of essentially human appearance and attributes, but own magical seal-skins which allow them to take the form of seals. Their society is tribal, and, except for the seal skins, much more primitive than Gaelic society in general. Most seal-people are on reasonably good terms with humanity, except for some tribes, which have a habit of raising storms when their members are killed by human seal-hunters. They are most likely of human origin[195].

**Spirit Animals:** Like human beings, the Daoine Síthe are said to keep livestock and other animals. These are usually said to be large, intelligent, and healthy specimens of their type, but not otherwise all that unusual. Such animals were regularly seen into the early twentieth century, and were often prized as breeding stock[196].

**Storm Spirits:** There are a variety of storm spirits in Gaelic folklore. A few are said to cause storms, but more often they warn mariners of dangerous weather. They occasionally appear as a misty human outline, but more often remain invisible. They are of unknown origin[197].

**Strangers:** The Strangers are a tribe of spirits found only in the Lincolnshire Cars, a swampy region in East-Central England. I include them here as example of: 1. An apparently independent tribe of spirits who take no part in the conflict between the Tuatha Dé Danann and their enemies; 2. An example of Celtic belief surviving among a people of English (ie. Ex-Celtic or non-Celtic) ethnicity; and 3. A form of Pagan folk-religion which survived, in direct competition with Christianity, into the late 19th century. Note that the Cars contain many other examples of such folklore, and are, for all intents and purposes, a study in themselves.

The Strangers are said to be small creatures, about one foot in height, with thin arms and legs, large feet, long noses, wide mouths, and long, prehensile tongues. Their clothing is green and their hats yellow. They otherwise have most of the abilities of the Daoine Síthe in general. The people of the Cars, who called themselves the "Fen-men", worshipped the Strangers for many generations[198]. The best description of their worship is given by an anonymous man, in M.C. Balfour's *Legends of the Cars,* though I first read it in Katherine Briggs' *The Vanishing People.* It was recorded sometime in the 1890s:

> O' summer nights they danced i' the moonshine on the great flat stones tha sees about; I don't know where they comes from, but my granther said how his granther's granther told him at long agone the folk set fire on the stones, an' smeared 'em wi' blood, and thought a deal more on 'em than of the passon bodies an' the Church……..

> In the gardens, the first flowers an' the first fruit an' the first cabbage, or what not 'ud be took to the nighest flat stone, an' laid there for the Strangers; in the fields, the first corn, or the first taters wor put to the tiddy people; and to hoam, afore they gan to yeat their vittles, a bit of bread an' a drop o' milk or beer wor spilled on the fireplace to keep the greencoaties from hunger an' thirst[199].

**Tree Spirits:** The spirits of trees are of various types depending on the tree. They may take almost any form, and range from the greatly hostile to the friendly and protective. In this, Gaelic folklore isn't really all that different from any other kind. Trees spirits are almost certainly of no other origin than from the trees themselves[200].

**Water Spirits:** A variety of spirits inhabit the lakes, rivers, and coastal waters of Ireland and Scotland. They take many forms, and range from neutral to friendly to humanity. They may be solitary beings, or, as among the Merrows, organized into complex societies. Many sightings or "sea serpents" or "lake monsters" may the sighting of the less human-like of these beings. They are of unknown, and likely of several different, origins[201].

# 3

# An Fhírinne

As we have already seen, the Tuatha Dé Danann have inhabited and guided this world since it was formed. It should come as no surprise, then, that they have established laws to govern this world, and that those laws are still operative today, even as in the earliest times. The traditional term for this Law is **Fírinne,** which has the meaning of Cosmic Truth. An Fhírinne denotes truth in a cosmic sense, the fitness of things, cosmic order, and the cycle of nature[1]. It implies the existence of the laws of nature, but also of a cosmic law in a more mystical sense. It is by Fírinne that the sun rises in the morning and the seasons move in their cycle. It is Fírinne which governs the growth of crops, the bounty of the forests and the sea, and the prosperity of the tribe.

But, Fírinne has an even more important social, personal, and ethical element. For, An Fhírinne includes not only the law of nature, but also the proper way of life established for human beings. As we shall see, Fírinne includes the social order established for the tribal community, the ethics whereby people can live in harmony with one another, and also the means whereby human beings can gain a good and fulfilling life[2].

## An Fhírinne on the Individual Level:

**The Basics:** When applied to the individual, Fírinne amounts to the way to live honorably and successfully. It is through following the precepts of Fírinne that one develops the habits of knowing oneself, living ethically, and working to achieve significant things that lead to both worldly and spiritual benefit and merit. The most basic, though not the only, element of living honorably is to be truly and authentically ourselves.

This is obtained only after a long and difficult road to self-discovery and self-mastery. We cannot truly be ourselves until we take the time to learn who we are, and how that person is meant to relate to others and to society. We can do this, by discovering the following elements of our souls:

1. **Dlúth:** Dlúth is a word denoting the inner nature of a person or thing. It literally refers to "warp" or "weave", and thus includes the concepts of a thing's essential make-up, and its relationship to the world as a whole[3]. At base, however, the Dlúth is **Who You Are.** It is your core identity, and your place in the world. Most all of the other elements of the soul arise from Dlúth, which survives physical death, and changes only very slowly, perhaps over the course of centuries, if at all. With very few exceptions, the Dlúth can only be discovered after years of searching, and often hard experiences in the world. There are no shortcuts to self-knowledge.

2. **Dán:** An Dlúth gives rise to Dán. Essentially, Dán is the Dlúth as expressed in each individual lifetime. It is also one of the most important words in a Celtic language. The concept of Dán is essentially a unified idea consisting of art, talent, destiny, fate, and vocation, in one[4]. It is the task set before you in this life, the "work" of this incarnation. In other words, it is **Who You Are Meant to Be.** Everyone has a Dán, which is to say, everyone has a place in this world. It is up to us to find out what that place is, and to fulfill it.

3. **Slí:** The word Slí simply means "way" or "path". It can be used in as many different ways in Irish as the word "way" can be used in English[5]. It can be used for the religion itself. It can be used for ethical conduct in general. It can be used for a path in the woods. In the phrase Slí Bheatha, it means "profession", what you do for a living. For our purposes in this chapter, it means the path set before you by your Dán. Each person has a path by which they may realize their Dán, and become who they were meant to be. As long as they stay on that path their lives will tend to flow in a beneficial way, and even their misfortunes will turn out eventually to their greater good. For this discussion, then, Slí is the **Path to Dán.**

**Cóir (core) – Ethics and Virtues:** The word Cóir comes from the Old Common Celtic "ko-wiria", meaning "with truth" and refers to the path of ethical and honorable conduct, to acting in accord with An Fhírinne. Ethical behavior, and right action are an inherent part of the cosmic order, built into the structure of the universe itself. People should act rightly for much the same reason that the sun rises in the morning: it is in their nature as human beings to do so. From this point of view, wrong action is not just disobedience of a divine commandment nor only causing harm to another. Rather, it is a violation of the divinely ordained structure of the universe.

Cóir also can be described in terms of **Na Buanna.** Buanna is the plural of the word **Bua**, which, as we shall see, has a complex meaning indeed. For our purposes right now, however, we can define Na Buanna as the moral virtues necessary to live a life of integrity, uprightness, truth, and goodness. It should be noted that this system of Buanna is taken from a post by Alexei Kondratiev entitled "Celtic Values", but has been modified somewhat by me over the years. The Buanna include:

1. **Dílseacht:** This word means loyalty to friends, family, Gods, and those to whom you have given your pledge. It means to be True, a true friend, a true child or sibling, true to others so that you can be true to yourself. The word is also used to refer to a dye that doesn't run, but keeps its color no matter what. This gives some shade of its meaning[6].
2. **Tairise:** This term refers to reliability, steadfastness, dependability. Once we know that you will be loyal to your friends, another logical question is: can they depend on you? Will you come through? Can others count on you? If they can, you have Tairise[7].
3. **Flaithiúlacht:** This term literally means "lordliness", but actually means generosity and lavishness. Will you give for others? Will you share with others? Will you provide for those who have less than you? This virtue is constantly referred to in the ancient Irish texts. Lords were praised for the feasts they gave, the gifts they bestowed, their open-handedness, their support for their tribe in hard times. It is especially important in the rich. In Gaelic society, to be rich, to have money, is not what makes one admired. It is **giving money away** that makes one admired[8].
4. **Aíocht:** A specialized form of Flaithiúlacht, this refers to generosity and hospitality toward strangers and the unfortunate. A stranger who came to an Irish home in ancient times could be assured of a place by the fire, and whatever of a meal that the host had available, with no questions asked. This was done because of the wildness of the country, and the distance between settlements. Today, the issues involved are a cold society that does not care for the poor and

unfortunate. We practice this virtue in modern times by giving our money or our time to help others, and even by giving to beggars[9].

5. **Ionraicas:** Uprightness, integrity. This is a person or thing that is honest, not flawed, the same on the inside as on the outside. In ancient times, it was used for goods that were sellable, undamaged, that were solid and good, in other words. In modern times, it means a person who is what he or she seems, who is incorruptible, just, and truthful. It is one of the greatest of virtues[10].

6. **Cneastacht:** An old term meaning sincere, whole, or healed, this refers to that aspect of Ionraicas concerning inner rectitude, and cultivation of the proper attitudes and emotions. To have Cneastacht is to be in a proper relationship with Fírinne in oneself. It is to feel and think appropriately[12].

7. **Macánta:** This is an old word meaning "the quality of a son". It refers to the gentleness, kindness, and guilelessness that noble-class Irish children were expected to learn. To have Macánta is to be gentle, kind, and willing to learn, from the low as well as the high[13].

8. **Misneach:** This word comes from an old term meaning "right measure", meaning "keeping things in perspective". It is used here to refer to a kind of courage. You have Misneach when you know that the most important thing is your own honor, integrity, and Gods, and when you are therefore able to face danger calmly, knowing that your fate is less important than your actions. A person with Misneach knows that he/she is mortal, and doesn't let danger upset him/her, but focuses on what is really important: dealing with the source of that danger in the best way possible[14].

9. **Calmacht:** This term means "hardness", but not in the sense of cruelty. It refers rather to hardness against pain, cold, hunger, and privation. It refers to endurance, the ability to bear discomfort in a higher cause without complaint or loss of spirit[15].

10. **Crógacht:** This term refers to ferocity, blood-thirst, and the ability to deal out wounds in battle. It means the ability to inflict pain, harm, and even death when truly necessary. Note that it is **very rarely** truly necessary to do this, but there are times when you must defend your family, when great injustices must be ended, or tyrants overthrown[16].

11. **Fios:** This term means wisdom or knowledge, specifically the knowledge of sacred or occult matters, the knowledge of virtue and of the soul. Without this knowledge, how will one know to act correctly? In modern Irish, the word survives as the general word for knowl-

edge or knowing, and no longer has any magical or occult shades of meaning[17].

12. **Dualgas:** This term means both "right" in the sense of civil or hereditary right, but also "duty". We can think of it as both one's rights and also duties in society, taken as a single, unified concept[18].

**The rewards of the Slí:** People who follow their Slí gain rewards. This is to say, that virtue is not all duty, but does result in a better life. Those who follow their Slí, including the Buanna, act in accord with the cycle and current of the universe, and so grow in power, knowledge, and status, among other things. The rewards of Slí are expressed in these two crucial concepts:

1. **Oineach:** Oineach means literally "face". More broadly, however, it refers to reputation, honor, achievement and social status. A person of high Oineach has achieved much, is honored by others, has a good reputation, and has risen in the social scale[19]. If you truly follow your Slí, then, others will in time notice. In time, you will be able to gain recognition, perhaps a bit of money, and respect for your achievements on the path. As we shall see, in an early Gaelic tribe, social status and wealth were given out on the basis of honor, and so the system of reward was more just than in modern society. In modern society, with a social system dominated by corporate interests, and undermined by its spiritual corruption, which rewards **having** more than **doing,** the system of honor is necessarily crippled and justice is often replaced by injustice. Even so, if you look around yourself, you will see that many, many strong and virtuous people are still able to gain Oineach.

2. **Bua:** We have already seen the plural of Bua used to refer to the virtues. In fact, the word is much more complex and important than that. Bua is a word that means, at one and the same time, virtue, victory, strength, and spiritual power[20]. Actually, there are more different kinds of spiritual power than Bua, but it is the most important of them, and the one it is possible to gain and lose by normal actions. We can perhaps think of Bua as a form of spiritual power that is accrued by virtuous actions, makes one stronger and more likely to act virtuously, and which brings victory and good fortune. People who have much Bua find their lives going mysteriously well. They are healthier and stronger. They are in the right place at the right time to get noticed and rewarded for their Dán. In addition, the more Bua you have, the more likely that you will act virtuously, bringing yet more Bua. Conversely, the more Bua you lose by acting wrongly, the harder it is to keep the Bua you still have.

**Bealach d'aimhleasa – the Bad Path:** It is, of course, not guaranteed that one will walk a good path in life. This is something up to us, and something we must choose. Many people choose to walk a bad path. The word for such a path is **Bealach d'aimhleasa**[21]. A Bealach d'aimhleasa is actually any way of life that is not in conformance with your own Slí. If one has a talent for painting, for example, but persists in trying to be a sculptor, no good can come of it. This is a form of Bealach d'aimhleasa. More commonly, the term is used to refer to "the road to ruin", to a bad path in general, a criminal life. It sounds like a cliché, but it is true that such lives lead nowhere. There are many millions of people who think they can live by theft, by cheating and swindling others, or by the violent abuse of others. Yet, if the realities of life are examined, it quickly becomes apparent that very few such people can succeed for very long. Most end up in prison, or killed by their rivals, or poor and abandoned by their "friends" once they are too old, sick, or weak to be of use. This is the natural result of walking a Bealach d'aimhleasa. The result of a Bealach d'aimhleasa is contained in the following concept:

1. **Diach:** This is a term for misfortune which results from following a Bealach d'aimhleasa[22]. It is similar to "bad karma" in that it is the natural, impersonal result of one's own actions. It differs from the idea of karma in that it is not on a one-to-one basis. Diach does not mean that if you hit someone, somebody else will hit you. It does mean that if you persist in living by dishonorable and selfish standards, there will be consequences until you change.

**Gessa (Gessa):** The word "gessa" is the plural of **Geis (gaysh),** a well known word referring to a variety of types of ritual prohibition or injunction[23]. There are many types of geis, actually, and the fact that gessa were used as a common plot-device has made untangling real gessa from fictional exaggerations difficult. In general, real gessa come in three types:

1. There are gessa which derive from one's Dlúth in some way. These are the strongest, and are often a by-product of the totemic relationships coming from a persons **fiorainm (fee-ur-awnnum),** which is to say, their true name, the name that reflects their Dlúth. For example Cúchulainn's true name means "Hound of Culann". He therefore had a geis against eating dog.
2. The second type of geis is derived from office or membership in a group. Often, this reflects totemic relationships of a particular family, tuath, or community. The best examples of these are the Gessa of kings and rulers, who represented their tuatha. In a few cases, there were apparently Gessa which effected entire tribes, though this

is quite rare, and not well understood in real history, as opposed to epic literature.

3. The term Geis could also be used for more ordinary vows. This is often seen in the epics, when someone "takes a Geis" to eat no food until they arrive at their destination, or something similar. Apparently, it was possible for one person to impose this sort of Geis on someone else. This should probably be regarded as nothing more than the assertion of a moral right, though it is a frequently employed plot device, which leads to various calamities which would suggest that it was taken very seriously. In general, the penalty for breaking a Geis of this third type is merely the shame and Diach that come from breaking an oath.

**Nascmhíol (Nawsk-veel):** The word Nascmhíol refers to a totem animal, that is, to an individual animal or animal species spiritually connected to a person's Dlúth, abilities, and well-being[24]. Generally, the Nascmhíol reflects the person in some way, according to the old Irish symbolic attributes of animals. So, a person who is a guardian may have the dog as a Nascmhíol; a person who is fast of foot and loves the woods may have the deer, and so on. In many old stories, at least some people are able to take the form of their Nascmhíol. One may or may not have the same Nascmhíol as one's patron deities:

**Beirmhíol (Bear-veel):** A Beirmhíol is a Nascmhíol obtained through the fiorainm. That is, the Beirmhíol is linked to a person through his or her true name. Generally, there is a geis against eating one's Beirmhíol. In most other respects, the Beirmhíol is similar to an ordinary Nascmhíol, though the connection is usually stronger[25].

**Claenmhíol (Clawn-veel):** The Claenmhíol is the totem of an entire family or tuath[26]. So, for example, the Tuath Ossoraighe had the deer as a Claenmhíol, the Múscraighe the elk, and so on. Generally, the link to a Claenmhíol is weaker than the link to an individual Nascmhíol, and there is usually not a geis against eating the animal's meat. The exception to this is the Ri or Tiarna of the tuath. As a living personification of the whole, the Ri or Tiarna has a geis against eating of the Claenmhíol, as well, usually, as many other gessa, which are sometimes very odd. Note that not every tuath or family has a Claenmhíol.

**Sacred Animals:** This is just a short list of the most common animals sacred in ancient Irish culture, and what they represented. Not every Nascmhíol will be on this list. There are as many types of Nascmhíol as there are animals in existence:

**Bear (Béar, pronounced as in English):** The bear is identified with strength, fertility, and the forest. In ancient Gaulish symbolism, a Goddess called Artio was identified with bears[27].

**Boar (Torc, Tor-uhk):** The Boar was the symbolic animal of the Otherworld. It symbolizes ferocity, strength, mystery, war, and chaos, among other things. It was by far the animal most valued for feasting, and for the "champion's portion" given to the most honored warriors. In myth, it is often a boar which lures heroes into the Otherworld[28].

**Bull (Tarbh, Tar-ev):** The bull is a symbol of fertility, strength, wealth, and battle. They were a distinctly male symbol, often with sexual overtones[29]. The term "bull of battle" can refer to a good fighter, but also can refer to a good lover. On the other hand, the bull was used in the **Tarbh feis,** or Bull Feast, a form of divination by which kings could be selected[30].

**Cow (Bó, pronounced as it is spelled):** The cow is a symbol of wealth, fertility, and female power[31]. Cows are sacred to Boann[32]. Cattle were one of the primary means by which wealth was measured[33]. A red cow, on the other hand, is a symbol of the Mórrígan[34].

**Crane (Corr, pronounced as it is spelled):** The crane is an ambivalent symbol. On the one hand, it is a symbol of the Otherworld, and Manannnan's Crane Bag is a potent magical treasure[35]. On the other, cranes were reputed to steal strength and courage, and so regarded as a bird of ill omen[36].

**Crow and Raven (Préachan [Prach-un] and Fiach [Fee-uch]):** Symbols of the Mórrígan, crows and ravens are birds of battle, but also bringers of prophecy. In the old traditions, to see a crow on the way to battle foretold a great slaughter. A crow with a bloody rag in its mouth foretold defeat. In general, crows represent the presence of the Mórrígan[37].

**Dog (Cú [coo], or Madra [maw-druh]):** A symbol of guardianship and healing, the dog is at times also associated with the Otherworld.

Mostly, the dog is the symbol of protective power, and of protective deities[38].

**Duck (Lacha, pronounced Law-chuh):** The duck is the symbol of the protective and curative power of the sun. It is often used in charms against the evil eye and hostile magic[39].

**Eagle (Iolar, pronounced oo-leer):** The Eagle is the primary symbol of war, courage, strength, and heroism[40]. It is also one of the animals sacred to Lugh, and has associations with light as a result[41].

**Goat (Gabhar [gour]):** Wild goats are one of the animals protected by the Cailleach Beara, a local form of Dánu/the Mórrígan who is associated with winter, snow, forests, and the night[42].

**Goose (Gé, pronounced gay):** The goose is a symbol of protection and aggression. The term "wild goose" can be used to refer to a wanderer[43].

**Horse (Ech [ech] or Capall [cap-ull]):** The horse is the primary animal associated with kingship, the Earth, and the Goddess Macha. The horse is a very holy animal[44].

**Salmon (Bradán [Braw-dan]):** The salmon was the symbol of wisdom, knowledge, and ancient lore. The salmon could also be a symbol of prosperity and general benevolence[45].

**Serpent (Nathair [Naw-har]):** The serpent has a dual role in ancient Irish symbolism. On the one hand, it a symbol of wisdom and hidden power. It can be associated with the Otherworld, immortality, and renewal, as one might expect of an animal which regularly sheds its skin, and lives in a hole in the ground. It is in this role that the serpent is invoked at Imbolc[46]. On the other hand, serpents can also be seen as the cruel, greedy guardians of sacred wells and similar treasures. In this role, they are more often called **peist (paisht)** than nathair, and are the equivalents of the dragons of later European lore[47].

**Stag (Carria [car-ree-yuh]):** Stags symbolize fertility, prosperity, and the forest. The regular growth and loss of antlers can be a symbol of the seasonal cycle. In the Scottish Highlands, the deer are sacred to the Cailleach Beara, who was said to herd them, with them as her cattle, and so represent winter, the earth, mountains, snow, night, and so on[48].

**Swan (Eala [al-uh]):** The swan is a symbol of purity, innocence, and love. The motif of the swan-maiden as a desirable young lover is as common in Ireland as in other European countries, and, indeed, around the world[49].

## Fírinne on the Social Level:

**The Tuath:** The **Tuath** is the basic institution that underlays the way of Fírinne in social practice. The structure of the ancient Irish family, of ancient Irish law, and the entire way of life is based in the Tuath as its natural matrix and setting[50].

So, then, what was or is the Tuath? So great an authority as Mackillop defines a tuath simply as a tribe, a folk, or a people[51]. A Tuath, then, is an autonomous group of people, with a common sense of kinship and spiritual identity. In ancient times Tuatha lived on a common piece of land, usually about the size of an American or Irish county, with which they spiritually bonded. The Tuath shares a common Tuath Éarlamh or Éarlaimh, usually an ancestor or land Goddess, or both. The leader of a Tuath is normally called the Ri, and embodies the Tuath in a ritual sense. In addition, there is a Tuath assembly, called an Oireacht, at which decisions are made by democratic means[52].

The power of the Ri derives not from either a God of heaven, as in many cultures, nor from the secular will of the people, as in most forms of modern political theory. Rather, the Ri derives his/her power to rule from the Macha, the Goddess of Sovereignty, and from the local Land Goddess, who can be seen as a form of Macha. Ultimately, the relationship between Tuath and Land is of central importance to Pagan Gaelic political thought. The Tuath can not prosper unless the Land is properly cared for, nor can a Tuath that abuses or pollutes the Land be regarded as having legitimate title to its own lands. In this sense, environmental concerns are directly part of Gaelic political theory[53].

Today, the term is, perhaps somewhat unfortunately, mostly used for the CR equivalent of a "coven", a group of at least two Irish Pagans who come together for worship and community. In this form, Tuatha, and the equivalents of Tuatha have flourished on the internet and to some extent in real life. Such groups do, however, allow us to practice the way of Fírinne in company with others, and to build at least he beginning of strong local institutions.

Unfortunately, many – not all, but many - groups claiming to be tuatha on the internet today are frauds, often consisting of a single person, usually male, and their computer. I have encountered "tuatha" claiming to be able to field 30 armed warriors, and to initiate young men by hunting boars with spears! Needless to say, all such claims are nonsense at best. When dealing with any such groups, whether over the internet or in person, one's best weapon is one's sense of skepticism. If any claims seem too good to be true, they almost certainly are. When you are wondering about such a claim, be sure to check it and make sure it is documented in such a way that the documentation cannot **under any circumstances** be faked by computer.

1. **Divisions of a Tuath:** The Tuath, then, can serve as a badge of identity, a community of Celtic Reconstructionists, in which the laws of Fírinne can be fulfilled and through which they can be expressed in the wider world. There are also a number of smaller units of Gaelic society, which can serve as divisions of a sufficiently large tuath, or the term for a local group for those who might desire such. These include the **Cineal, Fine, Neimheadh,** and **Teallach.**
    a. **Cineal:** The word Cineal means "kindred", and essentially refers to a kin-group living in the same area or district. Indeed, in later times the term was often applied to districts ruled by a particular family.54. In modern times, we can use it as an assembly or community of Celtic Pagans who live in the same town or rural area. This would likely include more than one Teallach (see below).
    b. **Fine:** This term means "family", or "family lineage". It was a very important unit in early Irish society for legal as well as social purposes. Indeed, the extended family retains its social importance in rural Ireland to this day55. A few organizations have used it as a term for a local cell. With respect, I would suggest that this term should be reserved for a real family, of whatever type, that has shared finances, children, and, preferably, a sense of not-necessarily hereditary lineage or shared ancestry to pass on to its descendants.
    c. **Neimheadh:** This term means "temple" or "sanctuary". It is used to refer to any space used for traditional worship, or, less often for ritual space generally56. We can also use it to refer to a Teallach that has dedicated a permanent neimheadh, including a full complement of temple officers, open for public worship and teaching.

d. **Teallach:** The word Teallach means "hearth". In modern times, we can use the term both to refer to a ritual hearth for sacred fires, and also to our version of a "coven", a group of at least two unrelated worshippers who come together for religious and cultural community.

**Oineach in the Tuath:** As we have seen, the word oineach refers to social status as well as to reputation, personal honor and achievement. This underscores the fact that a tuath is a hierarchical society, ranked according to the honor, knowledge, and achievements of its members[57]. Justice consists not in treating everyone the same, but giving to each person what he or she is due[58]. In ancient times, there were a number of different systems of rank recognized at different periods, and in different parts of Ireland. They shared a tendency to rank people by age and property, with the older and richer having more status than the younger and poorer[59]. In part, this was due to the nature of early Irish inheritance law, which made reasonably certain that every member of a Fine would inherit when a wealthy member died, so that the ancient Irish had a strong tendency to rise through the social scale as they aged[60]. In addition, status was very much dependent on skill in war, and on one's conduct.

In more modern times, we would find it quite difficult to go back to being communities of warrior-farmers, ranked by wealth and valor. Nor should we. Such communities would tend to thoroughly alienate their neighbors, and would, in consequence of their makeup, likely be too weak to survive when those neighbors made their displeasure known. In an age of smartbombs, nuclear warheads, and powerful states that look with a jaundiced eye on well-armed rural warrior compounds, to return to the heroic age lifestyle would be suicidal.

Nor would it truly serve our interest. Our task today is cultural revival, the spread of knowledge. We need a system of rank that rewards people for **learning**, and for **producing** the stuff of culture. Luckily, we can adapt the social system to this purpose, witout doing too much violence to it, by rewarding teaching and study. We can use the ancient system of ranks, in part accurately, reflecting the number of one's clients, and in part to reflect levels of access to tribe membership based on learning and trust. In addition, we can use the ranks of learned persons (the *Aes Dána)*, to give ranks to those who keep alive traditional learning and culture.

Such a system of ranks might look as follows:

1. **Fuidir:** In ancient times, a *fuidir* was a serf, a person not a member of the tuath who was allowed to farm land by a noble in exchange for labor service and a large portion of his or her crops. Today, we can use the term for an untried student, one who is still new to the tuath and has not fully assimilated the values of Gaelic culture, and so cannot be trusted to behave honorably. Such a fuidir has a master, who in this context would be a teacher, expected to tutor the newcomer in the ways of the tribe and the values of Irish Paganism. They would have no real rights in the tribe, but conversely, could not be held responsible for their actions, until they had some clear understanding of how to live honorably.
2. **Feine:** The term *feine* referred in ancient times to a free farmer, a full tribe member. Today, we can use it for full members of the tuath, who have full rights. There are two ranks of feine:
    a. **Ogaire:** A term meaning "young lord", we can use this rank to refer to people who are full tribe members, but as yet young and inexperienced. Most people would hold this rank for their first year or so in the tribe, and would advance to higher rank by showing commitment to the tribe by attendance at functions, proper behavior, and taking a role in tuath affairs.
    b. **Boaire:** A term meaning 'cattle lord', *boairig* were the free owners of cattle in early Gaelic society, often neither having clients nor being clients themselves. We can use the term for the full, respected tribe member, the backbone of the tuath.
3. **Aes Dana:** Ancient Gaelic societies had a class of people, in part hereditary, in part adopted, devoted to keeping the traditions, lore, arts, crafts, and histories of the various tuatha and of Gaelic culture as a whole. These people were called **Aes Dána**, which translates as "people of art". The Aes Dána were clergy, as well as professionals, and they were expected to be fully qualified for their positions[61]. Divisions or specializations of the Aes Dána included the **Draoid** (Druids or clergy proper), **Filid** (traditional poets, *in the Irish language*), **Seanchaid** (academic-level historians and genealogists), **Faith** (seers or diviners), **Brithim** (legal specialists), **Liaig** (certified healers, herbalists, and medical professionals), and **Ceolteori** (traditional Celtic musicians)[62]. The Aes Dána were ranked by their years of study and mastery. We can use that system of ranks today, as follows:

a. **Fochlac:** One or fewer years of study. Equivalent in rank to an Ogaire.
b. **Mac/Ni Fuirmidh:** Two to three years of study. Equaivalent in rank to a Boaire.
c. **Dos:** Three to four years of study. A learned, respected man or woman of high character, equivalent in rank to a Féar Fothla.
d. **Cana:** Four to five years of study. This would probably be someone studying for the clergy, and qualified to practice healing, herbalism, and so on. Equivalent in rank to an Aire Deso.
e. **Cli:** Five to eight years of study, or Bachelor's Degree in field, plus proven competence. The lowest clergy level. Equivalent in rank to an Aire Ard.
f. **Anradh:** Eight to twelve years study, or accredited Master's Degree in field, plus proven competence. More honored clergy. Equivalent in rank to an Aire Tuise.
g. **Ollamh:** More than twelve years study in field, or accredited Doctorate, plus proven excellence. This is the level of a true Master, who has earned his or her rank by real, demonstrable study and hard work. Equivalent in rank to the Aire Forgill.

4. **Aire:** In ancient times, the *airig* were the nobility, the great warriors and landowners, with many clients. Today, we use the term to refer to those who are qualified to teach our values, who do teach our values, and who take it on themselves to lead and to guide others. Modern airig are tribe members of distinction, people of accomplichment, proven honor, and great worth. There are a number of sub-ranks based on the number of one's students:
   a. **Fear Fothla:** This is the lowest rank of aire, and refers to a person of great and proven honor, who is able to teach, but as yet has fewer than five current and former students.
   b. **Aire Deso:** This is an aire with five free clients, probably former students, and five students.
   c. **Aire Ard:** This is a higher-ranking aire, with ten free clients, and ten students.
   d. **Aire Tuise:** This is an aire of great distinction, with 15 free clients, and 15 students.
   e. **Aire Forgill:** This is the highest ranking Aire Tuise in the tuath, and therefore the highest ranking aire in the tuath except for the *rí*. If a tuath does not have Airig Tuise, then it probably has no need for an Aire Forgill.
5. **Ríghdamhna:** In ancient times, these were people of royal rank, the highest level of tribe leadership. So it is today:

a. **Tanaise Rí:** The designated successor to the rí. Note that the Tanaise Rí does not automatically become rí on the death of resignation of the sitting rí. Rather, the Tanaise must be confirmed and approved by the Oireacht, the assembly of tuath members.
b. **Rí:** The rí is the leader of the tuath, approved by its members, and given the power of *flaitheas* by Macha. The rí is responsible for maintaining the honor of the tuath itself, and for being the living embodiment of the tuath in a ritual sense.[63]

**Céilsine (Kel-shinn-uh) – Cliency:** Cliency was the means by which the ancient Irish nobility maintained order in the Tuath, provided channels for political debate, and redistributed wealth. It at once maintained the power of the elite, and prevented that power from getting out of hand and trampling the rights of the average tribe-members. For the elite, cliency provided (more or less) loyal followers, a way of resolving differences among themselves in a (more or less) nonviolent way, a means of control over the resources of the Tuath, and a means of enforcing the laws and other social norms. For the average tribe member, cliency provided protection from crimes and abuses, the ability to lobby the nobility, and a source of stock, seed, and wealth which would not have been otherwise obtainable[64]. There were two types of cliency:

**Saor Céilsine:** Saor céilsine means free cliency, cliency without restrictions on liberty. In the old texts, a free client received three cows from a lord, for a seven year period. For the first three years he or she owed one cow per year. For the second three years, the lord received the equivalent of one cow's value per year in milk products, calves, and dung (used as fertilizer and, when dried, as fuel). In the seventh year, the client had to either return the cattle, or enter into the agreement of cliency again. All free clients owed homage, which meant that they had to rise to their feet in the presence of their lords, or, if already standing, raise one knee, as well as support their lords in the tribal assemblies. In addition, they owed roughly one labor-service per year, which amounted to helping the lord with the harvest for a few days. The lord not only had to give the cattle, but also had to support their clients on the assembly and in legal disputes unless there was clear and good cause not to. Although lords of free clients did not have to protect their clients against attack, or avenge attacks on them, they usually did. Note that free clients could end their cliency at any time, merely by returning the cattle, without penalty. Note also that most free clients were blood relatives of their lords[65].

**Daor Céilsine:** Daor céilsine means "base" or unfree cliency, cliency with restrictions on liberty. Most base clients received their honor price from their lord, in cattle or other livestock, and often much more. In addition, symbolically, the lord gave to his base clients a double-handed vat and a cauldron, which apparently meant something to the effect of "your food comes from me". The base client owed the equivalent of one third the value of the amount loaned per year in both livestock and processed foods (ie. smoked hams, bread, and so on), labor service at harvest (for which the lord owed a harvest banquet in return), support in the assembly and in legal disputes, military service, work on the lord's rath and tomb, and support of the lord and his/her retainers when they traveled about the tribal territory, especially during times of war. The lord in turn now had a legal obligation to keep his/her clients from harm or hunger, to prosecute or avenge all injuries done them, to support them in disputes, and to pay compensation should they do injury to others. Contracts of base cliency lasted seven years, and base clients were not free to end these contracts during that time. They could, however, end the contract at the end of the seven years by returning the livestock lent. It was comparatively easy for a base client to borrow livestock from one noble in order to pay off another, thus changing lords. In fact, lords gained so much in status, wealth and real power from having clients that there was constant competition for clients, free and base alike. In this way, clients often played lords off against one another to get the best terms66.

**Céilsine Today:** In modern times, we are mostly not farmers, nor do we live at an Iron Age level. The specific problems of different levels of agricultural wealth which the system of céilsine is designed to address are not ours. We do, however, have several other problems, for which a much modified version of the system might prove helpful. Specifically, we have, or will have, in our groups the need to transmit knowledge so that new members may be properly assimilated into our tribes, and so that the disruption of new people, and the infiltration of modern values is reduced as much as possible. It seems to me that we could term new students who are of fuidir rank and not yet versed in the ways of our society and religion as daer ceilte to those who would teach them. The lord would thus undertake to teach his or her student the basics of Irish Paganism, most especially the values and social skills of living in an honorable way according to the buanna. Such people would not be given either rights or responsibilities except to learn, until such time as they showed they could use those rights and responsibilities in ways that were not disruptive to the tuath. After initiation into the tuath, tribe members could choose to remain saer ceilte to their teachers as a gesture of respect, and a way of helping their teacher attain greater rank, or they could assign this allegiance to another, more respected lord, or to no one as they chose. This would then become a mechanism for determining which leaders were the most respected, and for giving them the greatest honors. It would also help the tribe determine which teachers were treating their students in ways that did or did not win the affection of those students over the long run.

**Lánamnas (Law-num-nus):** This is the Irish word for marriage[67]. It is quite different from the Anglo-American version of marriage, almost amounting to a different institution. It should be noted that, although the Brehon Laws are no longer in force, it is fully compatible with modern marriage laws in most places, and can be re-instituted, to at least some degree.

**Making of Marriage:** A marriage, under the Brehon Laws, required more than merely a ceremony, or even a license. There were/are four primary ingredients: coibche, tionscra, a contract, and a ceremony. All are needed for a true marriage.

**Coibche (kiv-shuh):** The Coibche is a price or gift given by the groom to the bride. Depending on the types of marriage, the coibche and tionscra may be of different sizes[68].

**Tionscra (Tinn-uh-scruh):** The Tionscra is a price or gift given by the bride to the groom. Both coibche and tionscra are usually placed into a joint account (in the old days, a single pasture!), and used to pay for various household expenses. Offenses by the bride against the groom or the groom against the bride (eg. infidelity) may be paid for by requiring the offender to pay an additional coibche or tionscra. If the marriage should end, each party is normally liable only for the coibche or tionscra, including increase due to interest, plus any jointly owned properties, unless there are reasons for the payment of an honor price[69].

**Contract:** The obligations of both parties, the type of marriage, and so on, are normally set out in a contract. In ancient times, such contracts were oral. Today they should be written, and be a legally binding prenuptial agreement that specifies the obligations of both parties during the marriage, including especially the care of children, and also guidelines for dissolution[70].

**Ceremony:** A marriage, of course, requires a marriage ceremony. The traditions here are only guidelines, for there was much variation in Gaelic marriage customs from age to age and place to place. A few common themes which I like are:
1. Often, the bride required the groom to perform some task to prove his sincerity and dedication. You find this a lot still in folk songs. Less commonly, the groom required this of the bride[71].
2. Sometimes there was a mock battle between the bride's family and the groom's men, which ended with the "abduction" or defection of the bride. This connects the marriage to seasonal mythology[72].

3. Usually, there were offerings to deities concerned with the household, family, and prosperity, especially Brigid and the Dagda.
4. Finally, the marriage itself could be symbolized by the bride giving a cup of mead to the groom to drain. This is connected to the myths of sovereignty and union between Gods and Goddesses[73].

**Types of Marriage:** There were actually ten types of marriage by the old laws. But only six of these mattered, and the other four were actually cumbersome ways to punish different types of sexual misconduct, or to deal legally with the consequences of promiscuous sex. The six which we need to worry about today, are as follows:

**Lánamnas Coimthinchuir (Law-mum-nus co-hin-chur):** The most respectable type of arrangement, this was a marriage between two partners with an equal coibche and tionscra, and the two setting up a joint household. A connection between people of equal status[74].

**Lánamnas Mná Foir Fearthinchur (Law-mum-nus Mnaw For Far-hin-chur):** This is an arrangement in which the woman contributes much less than the man; that is, the tionscra is much smaller than the coibche. Here, the man is of greater status, and so head of the household[75].

**Lánamnas Fir Foir Beantinchur (Law-mum-nus Feer For Ban-tchin-chur):** This is the opposite if the above, an arrangement in which the man contributes much less than the woman. In this case, the coibche is much smaller than the tionscra. Here, the woman is of higher status, and so head of the household[76].

**Lánamnas Airite Foir Úrail (Law-mum-nus Awr-ich-uh For Oo-roil):** This is the pure concubine, a woman who gives no tionscra, and the coibche the same as her honor price. The husband has the rights of an aire over a ceile. Such a woman was termed an **adaltrach,** said term being an obvious Christian loanword, or, more politely and accurately, a **bean-urnadna.** This one is probably harder to make legal, depending on local laws and customs[77].

**Lánamnas Fir Foir Beantinchur....Fear Fognama (Law-mum-nus Feer For Ban-tchin-chur Far Fo-naw-vuh):** Despite its name, this is the opposite of the Lánamnas Airite Foir Urail. In this marriage, the man gives no coibche, and the woman pays a tionscra equal to his honor price. The wife has therefore the rights of an aire over a ceile, and, in addition, the man had to perform labor service for her. Such a man may have been called a **fear-urnadna,** though I have never actually seen the term[78].

**Lánamnas Fir Thathigte, gan Targuid, gan Urgnam (Law-mum-nus Feer Haw-higthe gawn Tawr-gooj, gawn Oor-nawv):** This was a marriage in which the two people did not form a single household, but were regular lovers. There would be only a token coibche and tionscra, with fewer obligations on either party. Again, this would be unlikely to be a legal marriage, but rather something more on the lines of "handfasting" in other Pagan traditions[79].

**Altramas (Awl-tramus) – Fosterage:** Fosterage was the custom of sending of children to be raised by other people, usually from the ages of seven to seventeen. It was a cornerstone of the society of the Gaelic upper classes, important to family relations, political alliances, and education. It was normal for the parents to pay to the foster-parents a fosterage fee, which could be forfeit if the child were abused. The treatment of foster-children was closely regulated by law, though it would seem very harsh by modern standards. Though beatings were rare, food and clothing were barely sufficient. Normally, the maternal uncle of the child became the foster-parent, though people of high rank sent their children to be raised by local rulers. In this latter case, the ruler maintained a well-organized system for caring for the children, in effect a boarding school, with a bent toward instruction in the military arts, a kind of military school, in short. In addition to instruction in fighting, the "boy troops" were taught many things by the Druids maintained in the ruler's court, particularly in the areas of literature, religion, poetic meters, astronomy, and courtly manners. It is very likely that fosterage among the less powerful people in society served as a kind of apprenticeship system, and was geared to teaching a trade or craft. However, we have so little data on this that it remains unclear. The term for foster-child in old Irish was **dalta (dawl-tuh),** which could also mean student. The terms for foster father and foster mother were **aite (awchuh)** and **muime (mmo-uh),** which meant "daddy" and "mommy" respectively[80]. I am uncertain what role, if any, fosterage could have today, though there may be circumstances of family distress where it is an appropriate and humane solution.

**An Fénechas – The Brehon Laws:** The Fénechas was the native term for the Irish code which has come to be known in English as the Brehon Laws. The two terms give very different impressions of the nature of these laws: the term Fénechas means "Law of the Land Tillers", and refers to the laws being the result of agreement of the people of the various tribes. The English term Brehon Laws refers to the Brithim, the class of professional jurists who administered, interpreted, and even changed the laws[81]. While no longer in force as a legal system, they do provide models for the bylaws of our organizations, and also living with one another according to An Fhírinne:
   A.   **The Books of the Law:** The Irish Laws were written down, at least from the time of Saint Patrick, and there are references in the *Life*

of *Saint Patrick* to written laws which he helped to reform, suggesting that written law codes are of even earlier date. There are many, many surviving law-books, written at different times, and in different places, which to some extent contradict one another. The most important are probably the *Seanchas Mór* (Shawn-uh-chus Mawr), supposedly written down by a committee chaired by Saint Patrick himself, and the *Book of Acaill,* of similar antiquity, though less august authorship. All of the law-books which survive are post-Christian in date, and are supposedly deliberately altered so as to be in conformity with Christian doctrine[82].

B. **Legal Status:** The legal status of persons was determined by their own oineach, any land they might own, and the legal status of their kin. This establishes their **log n'oineach**, or honor price, as well as their ability to swear oaths[83].

C. **Offenses:** The Fénechas recognized a number of types of offences, with consequent penalties:
  1. **Types of Offense:** There were two main classes of offenses, offenses against people and offenses against property:
     a. **Offenses Against People:** Offenses against people included crimes like murder, injury, rape, and sexual harassment, among other offenses, as well as matters of honor such as libel, refusal of hospitality, and violation of hospitality[84].
     b. **Offenses Against Property:** Offenses against property included animal trespass, human trespass, damage to buildings or movable property, and theft, among other offenses[85].
  2. **Law of Compensation:** The Fénechas was almost purely a law of compensation, and not a law of retribution, as are most modern legal systems. That is, the task of the law was not to punish the wicked, but to ensure that the victims of crimes were compensated, and that wrongs were made right. This meant that the Irish laws were essentially a long list of possible offenses, with the fines for each, to be paid by the offender to the victim. There are two main types of fine, and usually both were paid by offenders:
     a. **Éric (ay-rik):** The term éric, in Old Irish, refers to a blood price, or a price for injury. All types of physical assault or injury, from minor assault to murder, had their accompanying éric. An éric was also paid for damage to property and theft, based on the worth of the property stolen, and the cost of repairing it[86].

b. **Log n'Oinach (Loy nyenech):** This is the honor price. With a very few exceptions, all crimes are assumed to involve insult as well as injury. The Log n'Oineach, then is the price of insult, arranged by the oineach rank of each person in the tribe. If a crime involved particularly heinous behavior, the Log n'Oineach could be increased to various multiples. In some cases, mostly libel, only a Log n'Oineach would be paid[87].

D. **The Institution of Troclaigh (Trok-lee), or Fasting:** We will not spend any time on court procedures, which could be complex in the extreme. With one exception. The institution of troclaigh was resorted to when a powerful person was judged against in a legal case and refused to pay. In this case, a person of lower status and power could seat him or herself in front of the offender's house and fast. If the faster should be allowed to die before the compensation was paid, the offender lost all oineach, *including* such legal necessities as oath-weight and Log n'Oineach. In this way, among others, the less powerful were protected from abuse by the more powerful[88]. The word troclaigh survives in the modern Irish word "trochlú", meaning "deterioration, breakdown, decay".

# 4

# The Otherworld

The idea of the Otherworld has long held a central place in ancient Gaelic thought, and also in later Gaelic folklore. Two categories of Irish story, Adventures (Echtrai) and Voyages (Imrama) concern themselves with visits to the Otherworld, or the intrusion of the Otherworld into mortal life[1]. The Otherworld also appears in the lore as a source of wisdom, the realm of the dead, and the home of the Tuatha Dé Danann[2]. Insofar as Celtic Paganism has "shamanistic" elements, these concern the Otherworld and the wisdom to be gained there[3].

The nature of the Otherworld is described differently in different sources. It is variously described as a realm of light, a realm of darkness, a place of joy, and one of sorrow, inhabited by beings as diverse as the Fomoire, Tuatha Dé Danann, and the human dead[4]. Indeed, so diverse are the descriptions that it is clear to me that we are actually dealing with a set of **Otherworlds** which together form an "exemplary model", a set of primordial realms from which all things in this world, whether beautiful or ugly, good or evil, pleasant or unpleasant, derive their meaning, and indeed their reality[5]. In this chapter, the particular Otherworld with which we will be concerned will be the realm often called Tír na'n Óg, the world inhabited by many of the Gods, and many of the human dead. From here on, the term "Otherworld" will be used to refer to this Otherworld only.

The location of the Otherworld is likewise variously described in different sources. Probably, the two most common conceptions are that the

Otherworld is under the Earth, frequently under a holy hill, or that it is over the sea[6]. Now and again, it is also said to be under water, the "Land Under Wave (Tír no Fhuin), though this term is less common and more often used to describe a specifically undersea realm inhabited by Merrows and other aquatic spirits[7]. It is interesting that the realm of the Fomoire is likewise variously described as being underground, across the sea, or under the sea, much as is the Otherworld itself[8]. This suggests that the various locations given to the Otherworld are meant to be taken as metaphor or allegory for the separation of the Otherworld from this realm[9]. It might be quite accurate to regard the Otherworld as being, in terms reminiscent of science fiction, a "parallel world".

**The Voyage to the Otherworld:** The Otherworld is at one and the same time close to and separated from the mundane realm. At certain times of the year, notably Samhain and Bealtaine, the two are so close that it is possible to move from one to the other without knowing. The Adventures most often concern such accidental journeys and their consequences[10]. Throughout most of the year, however, formidable barriers exist between the two, which require both bravery and wisdom to cross. These barriers are usually termed the **Idircheo,** meaning "between mists", though they entail much more than mist. The Voyage tales concern attempts to cross the Idircheo, though they are much modified by the Irish literati's deliberate imitation of various Biblical tales, and, even more, the Odyssey. Probably closer to the original native tradition are a number of old poems and ballads, of which the most important is probably "The Ballad of Thomas Rhymer", which preserves elements of fantastic antiquity, for all that it was not composed in a Celtic language, but instead in Scots English. Most of these sources contain a number of common elements, which allow us to reconstruct what an Otherworld journey entails[11].

One of the most important elements in the Voyage-type journey is the Guide. The Guide to the Otherworld can take any of a variety of forms, but always introduces the idea of a spiritual realm, and gives instructions on how to get there[12]. In the "Voyage of Bran (Imram Brain)", for example, the Guide is a beautiful woman called the "woman from unknown lands", who describes the Otherworld to Bran, and instructs him immediately to set out to sea. Bran also meets Manannán mac Lir on this journey, who takes the role of a Guide by telling Bran that he is near his goal[13]. In the "Ballad of Thomas Rhymer", the Guide is the Queen of the Síthe, who approaches Thomas, takes him up behind her on her horse, and rides away with him to the Otherworld[14].

It is interesting that Manannán should appear as a Guide in one of the Voyages, but not really very surprising. Indeed, Manannán is much more than a sea-God, and possesses vast knowledge of the ways from one world to another[15]. Manannán indicates that his ability to travel is at least in part magical in nature when he tells Bran that:

> Bran deems it a marvelous beauty
> In his coracle on the clear sea;
> While to me in my chariot from afar
> It is a flowery plain on which he rides about[16].

This, of course, indicates that Manannán travels, in part, by shifting his consciousness so that he sees the world in a non-ordinary way which allows him to work by different rules. In effect, he is able to ride on the sea in his chariot because, to him, it is not the sea.

The Otherworld, even if underground, is separated from this world by a body of water, or some other liquid. In the Voyages of Bran, Mael Dúin, the Uí chorra, and of Snédgus mac Riagla, this body of water is the ocean, and the Otherworld is pictured as an island[17]. In the Voyage of Laoigire, this body of water is Loch Naneane, in County Roscommon, into which he dives with fifty supporters on his journey[18]. In the Ballad of Thomas Rhymer, we read:

> For forty days and forty nights
> They wade through red blood to the knee
> And he saw neither sun nor moon
> But heard the roaring of the sea[19].

That this body of water is not to be confused with the ordinary ocean is confirmed by the fact that it is a sea of blood in Thomas Rhymer. It is, perhaps, more like the vast darkness reported by survivors of Near Death Experiences: a barrier between this world and another[20].

Between this world and the Otherworld, travelers will often encounter still other realms or worlds, many of them strange or dangerous. One such realm in the Voyage of Bran is the Island of Mirth, where the travelers find a great crowd of people, all laughing and gaping at nothing[21]. In the Voyage of Mael Dúin, there are more than thirty such worlds, including islands of mirth, of sorrow, islands with various structures on them, and islands with various inhabitants, some quite monstrous. Many of these are clearly meant to imitate episodes in the Odyssey. Others are taken from the Bible, and still others are clearly intended as philosophical allegory. In Thomas the Rhymer, this element takes the form of the poisoned garden from which Thomas must not eat. Without the Guide, who not only warns him, but supplies him with food and drink, Thomas might well have been tempted by the succulent fruit of the garden and been lost[22].

In the Ballad of Thomas Rhymer, we find another element of the Otherworld journey, though one less common in the surviving literature, the Two Paths, which here are actually three:

> Oh, so you see that broad, broad road
> That lies by the lily leven
> Oh that is the road of wickedness
> Though some would call it the road to heaven.
>
> And do you see that narrow road
> All beset with thorns and briars
> Oh that is the way of righteousness
> Though after it but few enquire.
>
> And do you see that bonny, bonny road
> Which winds about the fernie brae
> Oh, that is the road to Elfland
> Where together you and I will go[23].

This example is clearly influenced by Christian ideas! However, also note the cunningly subversive element: the road to Elfland is a **Third** road, neither of righteousness nor wickedness, neither of God nor the Devil. This slyly undermines one of the basics of Christian belief: that there is only one way to or type of salvation. The Queen of Elfland is setting herself up as a **Third Force** within the Judeo-Christian world, and as an independent source of a kind of salvation and eternal life. There are many analogous themes in the Otherworld journeys of other Indo-European cultures – including Teutonic, Greco-Roman, and Vedic Indian Religions, among others. Often, in cultures without Christian influence, the two paths lead to the world of the Gods and the world of the dead, respectively, or, in some cases, to the Underworld, and the Sky-World[24].

**The Nature of the Otherworld:** Whether reached after a long and perilous voyage, or blundered into on Samhain eve, the Otherworld immediately presents the voyager with a set of conditions radically different from those of the mundane realm. These characteristics are both negative and positive, in that, taken together, they define both what the Otherworld, and is not. In general, they paint a picture of a way of life so different from, and superior to, our own as to be almost incomprehensible to us[25].

The negative characteristics are among the most important to our understanding of it. By "negative" I mean here not the unpleasant characteristics, but instead those aspects of ordinary existence which are **not** present in the Otherworld. These include the lack of time, the lack of climate change, and the lack of treachery, sadness, disease, and death[26].

The lack of time in the Otherworld is one of its defining features. Time does not exist in the Otherworld in the measurable, precise sense that it does in the mundane world. A visit to the Otherworld that seems to last for a few days might actually last for centuries, or a year in the Otherworld might take up only a few minutes of normal time. This lack of correspondence in time and space is called **iloireadas (il-or-uh-jus)** in Irish[27]. We can see this principle in action in the Voyage of Bran, when we are told that, though Bran's visit to the Isle of Women seemed to last only one year, "it chanced to be many years"[28]. When, after growing homesick, Bran and his men return to Ireland, they find that so long a time has passed that they are remembered only in legend[29]. In the Adventure of Nera we see the opposite case. After being in the Otherworld more than a year, Nera returns to the mundane world to find that the cauldron containing the Samhain feast has not yet begun to boil. Only a few minutes of mortal time have passed[30].

The lack of climate change, indeed, of climate in almost any sense, is another hallmark of the Otherworld. Essentially, the seasonal cycle, which is such an important part of our lives, does not exist in the Otherworld, which experiences only a single season. In most accounts, this is a perpetual summer, though an everlasting winter, spring, or autumn are not unheard of. We see an example of this in the Adventure of Nera, who proves he has been to the Otherworld by bringing with him summer foliage on Samhain eve[31].

The lack of treachery, sadness, disease, and death is another characteristic feature of the Otherworld, which is beyond all of the unpleasant features of human life, whether created by other people, nature, or the passage of time. We see this most clearly in the famous passage from the Voyage of Bran, which describes the Otherworld:

> Not known is wailing, nor treachery
> In the well-known, cultivated land.
> There is nothing rough or harsh
> But only melodious music striking the ear.
> Without sorrow, without gloom, without death,
> Without any sickness, without debility,
> That is the mark by which Emain is known[32].

In many other accounts, we find this same feature. The Otherworld visited by Oisín is described in these terms: "(neither) death nor decay shalt thou see."33 Similarly, the land visited by Connle, son of Conn of the Hundred Battles, is noted for the lack of the passage of time, death, or any of the processes of decay34.

The positive characteristics of the Otherworld tell us what it is. They establish the essential facts of life in the Otherworld, which determine the quality of the experiences of visitors and inhabitants alike. These characteristics include intense beauty, haunting music, inexhaustible if sometimes unusual food, perfect lovers, and the special role of truth.

The intense physical beauty of the Otherworld is perhaps its most commonly described attribute. Its trees are covered in blossom and fruit at once. Its grass is lush, its waters clear as crystal, its ground covered with blossom. In many accounts, the presence of inexhaustible light is said to be a feature of the Otherworld. In a few of them, this light is referred to as a **lack of darkness**, something paralleled in many accounts of Near Death Experiences35. The beauty of the Otherworld is clearly described in the story of Oisin:

> It is the most delightful country to be found, of greatest repute under the sun, trees drooping with fruit and blossom, and foliage growing on the tops of boughs36.

Another description of the Otherworld is contained in the Voyage of Saint Breandán. It combines Gaelic and Christian symbolism, but presents the classic Otherworld features with great lyrical beauty:

> Having passed almost an hour, as vast light surrounded us, and a land appeared – spacious, grassy, and extremely fruitful.......we saw no plant without flowers, or trees without fruit......even the stones themselves were of the precious variety.......37

The music of the Otherworld is also well-known for its beauty, and for its haunting quality38. In the Voyage of Bran, the music is not only a characteristic feature of the Otherworld, but also introduces it. It was a strain of this melody which lulled Bran to sleep, after which he awakened to find the silver branch which called to him the Woman from Unknown Lands39.

Otherworld music is generally agreed to be slow, plaintive, and lulling. Often, it lacks the structural features typical of more formal Bardic composition. Many types of Celtic traditional music are said to have their origin in the

Otherworld, including especially the planxty tunes of the 17th century musician Turlough O'Carolan[40]. In the Voyage of Laogire and MacCrimthann, the "sweet sounding music of the sídhe", is presented as so fulfilling that it is a major reason for Laogire to remain in the Otherworld[41].

The inexhaustible Otherworld banquet is a constant theme in Gaelic myth and literature. Like the contents of the Dagda's cauldron, it does not diminish, no matter how much is eaten, perhaps symbolizing the **absence of want** in the Otherworld as much as the presence of dishes that are nowhere clearly described[42]. Otherworld food was said in a number of texts and oral traditions to possess a number of very unusual features. In Irish folklore, Otherworld food is often said to trap those who eat it. To eat of it is to cease being a visitor, and to become a permanent resident of the Otherworld[43]. The Feast of age, given by Goibhniu from pigs manufactured by him, or perhaps given by Manannán, has a less sinister quality. To eat of it is to become immortal, impervious to either age or decay[44].

The pleasures of love and sexuality are often attributed to the Otherworld. Both men and women who travel to the Otherworld often find lovers there who are physically perfect, skilled partners, excellent conversationalists, and interesting people. So pervasive was the Otherworld's reputation for love that it is sometimes called Tir na Mban, meaning "Land of Women"[45]. While we do not find the term "Land of Men" attributed to the Otherworld, such examples as the Cornish tale of Cherry of Zennor indicate that the Otherworld lover was a pleasure open to women as well as men[46].

There are many illustrations of the romantic pleasures of the Otherworld in the vernacular literature. In the Voyage of Laogire and MacCrimthann, we find the following description:

> The noble plaintive music of the Sídhe,
> Going from kingdom to kingdom
> Drinking from burnished cups,
> Conversing with the loved one.
> My own wife
> is Fiacha's daughter Der Greine
> Also as I may tell you,
> (there is) a wife for every man of my fifty.
> One night of the nights of the Sídhe
> I would not give for your kingdom[47].

The importance of Truth in the Otherworld is illustrated in the story "How Cormac's Cup of Gold was Found". According to this story, a man came to Cormac mac Art on the rampart of tara and promised him a silver branch in exchange for the granting of three requests. When Cormac agreed, the man requested his wife, daughter, and son. Cormac was forced by his honor to let the man have his way, but set our in pursuit with his army as soon a the oath was fulfilled. After a short while, the army was engulfed in a great mist, and Cormac eventually found himself alone in a palace with a handsome couple. The couple fed Cormac from a pig which had the property that it could not be cooked unless a truth were told under each corner of it. During the feast, they drank from a cup which would split into three parts if three lies were told over it, and could only be restored by the telling of three truths. After this, the man revealed that he was Manannán mac Lir, who had led Cormac into the Otherworld in order to give him the cup which could tell lies from truth, and the branch for his enjoyment. Presumably, Cormac was allowed to return to Tara after that, with his wife, children, and new-found treasures[48].

# 5

# Na Fomoire

**Basics:** The old traditions are quite clear that the Tuatha Dé Danann are not the only race of powerful spiritual beings. As we have already mentioned, there are other races of spiritual beings, among them such peoples as the Fir Bolg, and the People of Neimheadh. The most feared and hated of spiritual races, and the special enemies of the Tuatha Dé Danann, are the **Fomoire**. The meaning of the word **Fomor** is unclear. It probably comes from two words meaning "under sea", but may also be derived from other words, essentially meaning "demon".[1] Other terms for the Fomoire, such as **Fachan**, have the clear connotation of negative beings, destructive spirits, so there is really no ambiguity about the nature of the Fomoire themselves. The Fomoire, then, are demonic spirits of darkness, enemies of the Gods, and the source of all unpleasantness in the ancient tales.

    A. Their Nature

**The Power and Nature of the Fomoire:** Like the Like the Tuatha Dé Danann, and the Daoine Síthe, among others, the Fomoire are essentially immaterial, as we understand the term, but able to take physical form. This may be any form in conformance with the Dlúth of the Fomor concerned. Usually, but not always, such forms are hideous in the extreme. Often, they appear in bizarre, demonic, or animal-like forms. Often, though by no means always, they are of dark color. More often, they have one arm, one leg, and one eye. This should not be confused with either racism or prejudice against the handicapped. When depicted in woodcuts and the like, the Fomoire are usually quite non-humainoid, bizarre creatures with almost bat-like faces, that show none of the bilateral symmetry associated with life as we know it. In short, they are completely alien and inimical to the normal, healthy life of our world.

Their powers are similar in both the old epics and in more recent folklore. They are able to send good and bad fortune, but show a marked preference for the bad. They can cause confusion, or make people get lost. They can spin illusions, and create various types of mental illness. More typically, they can send storms and natural disasters, usually to whole communities. Even more commonly, they send disease, usually large epidemic or pandemic diseases. They are, in short, the spirits of plague, madness, and calamity.2

**The Psychology of the Fomoire:** Why do they do it? What compels these beings to cause such evil in the world? The short answer appears to be that each one does it for him/her/itself. The Fomoire are apparently totally opposed to the cosmic order of An Fhírinne. They reject the notions of Dlúth, Dán, Bua, and, ultimately, of Fírinne itself. They reject the whole concept of honor or morality, of civility or respect for others. Each is wholly out for him/her/itself, with no concern for anyone or anything else. A defining characteristic of the Fomoire is their greed. They seem to have bottomless appetites, for power, wealth, pleasure, sacrifices, dominance. In a sense they are wholly and nearly irredeemably addictive, in that their appetites are beyond control, and beyond balance or any possibility of harmonious coexistence with other beings. Such bottomless appetite leads Fomoire to bully, loot, and despoil other beings, in order to feed their endless cravings. They lay waste to the world, yet are never satisfied themselves, and always need more. Though they sacrifice everything to their greed, including their ethics, honor, and relations with others, the very nature of that greed keeps them from ever being satisfied.

**The Society of the Fomoire:** Such beings get along neither with one another, nor with those foolish enough to worship them. Fomorian society is a constant struggle of each against each, a war that can never be won. It is, in addition, a tyranny, the brutal rule of the stronger over the weaker, in which the weak have neither rights nor recourse. While Fomorian society arranges itself into a pyramid, it is constantly in turmoil, and continually unstable, as each Fomor struggles to rise in the hierarchy and oppress his/her/its fellows. The leaders of the Fomoire, including **Crom Dubh,** their ultimate ruler, strive for total control of Fomoire and others alike, but the rank and file struggle to do as they would, and to satisfy their own bottomless cravings. The result is something like the archetypal totalitarian system – brutally repressive, under constant surveillance, rife with betrayal, and much more unstable and chaotic than the leaders want to admit. Unlike human societies, this system is not ameliorated by such institutions as the family, true friendships, or love. To call such a society a dystopia is to understate its horror and oppression.

**Crom Dubh, the Fomorian King:** In Lebor Gabala and Cath Mag Tuired, Fomorian society is presented as having many kings, with no good way to tell who is the strongest.3 More recent folklore, however, and a correct literary analysis of the ancient texts, including the two above, allow us to identify **Crom Dubh** as the strongest and most ruthless of the Fomorian rulers, the real ruler of the Fomoire. Crom Dubh, whose name means "The Bent Black One", is also called Crom Cruaich ("the Bent One of the Mound"), Balor, and Iuchar, among other names.4 He appears in myth as an evil giant with an eye that strikes people dead if he should just look on them, a bent figure to whom human beings were offered, and, often, as a large, dark, threatening animal, most often a bull, boar, dragon, or wolf.5 He appears to combine two roles: the tyrant king with the devouring monster. As tyrant king, he is the archetypal oppressor, who recognizes no rights nor limits, and seeks absolute control over all he rules. He is the ruler who rules by force and terror, by torture and treachery. He is the archetype of Hitler, Stalin, and all the other tyrants of history. As the devouring monster, Crom Dubh epitomizes the greed and bottomless appetite of the Fomoire themselves. He is the wolf that will eat you all up, the dragon that lays waste the fields, the force of chaos and destruction that must be stopped if life is to continue. He is not any particular kind of animal, and no animals may be identified with him. It is not an animal's species that identifies it with Crom Dubh, but rather its threatening nature.

**Gó, the Cosmic Principle of the Fomoire:** Gó (pronounced go), is the cosmic principle for which the Fomoire and Crom Dubh stand, the ultimate distillation of their ethos. Essentially, Gó is Cosmic Falsehood, in the same sense that An Fhírinne is Cosmic Truth.6 It denotes falsehood, deception, the unnatural, chaos, disease, pollution, and, perhaps, above all, betrayal as a way of life. It implies the negation of both natural and moral law, the denial of the rights of others, and the elevation of pure selfishness as the only aim of life. It implies needless conflict, conflict driven by the desire to dominate or to enslave others. It implies disrespect, for truth, for others, for oneself.

The nature of Gó as essentially unnatural tells us something very important about the Fomoire. **The Fomoire are *not* Nature Spirits.** They do not dwell in nature. Indeed, they largely hate and despise nature, and the state of harmonious balance which it represents. Instead, they dwell in places where Gó is present, polluted places and places where great crimes have occurred. A few dwell in distant waste places where the power of Fírinne is weak for various reasons, as well. Almost no Fomor, however, would or could dwell in a normal, natural landscape.

**An Domhain, the Realm of the Fomoire:** Like the Tuatha Dé Danann Danann, the Fomoire dwell in another world, parallel to this one, yet separated from it. This world is called An Domhain, which has the meaning of "the Abyss".[7] Like the Otherworld of Tír na'n Óg, An Domhain is separated from this world by the Idircheo. Like the Otherworld, it grows closer to this world at Samhain and Bealtaine, when it is possible to enter it accidentally. Like the Otherworld, it presents those who enter it with a radically different set of conditions from those prevailing in the more mundane realm. Those conditions, however, also differ from those of the Otherworld itself.

Of the negative characteristics of the Otherworld, the only one that also applies to An Domhain is the lack of time. An Domhain is also outside the circle of time, and therefore behaves similarly to the Otherworld as regards the duration of events and stays within it. Unlike the Otherworld, An Domhain has plenty of climate, usually of the worst kind. Visits to the Land of the Fomoire usually include descriptions of fog, rain, and moisture of all kinds. Often, An Domhain is depicted as being in the cold depths of the sea, in which case it is often confused with such other realms as Tir no Fhuinn or the realm of the Merrows. Cold goes along with wet in descriptions of An Domhain's climate. Likewise, the lack of sadness, treachery, disease, and death does not seem to apply to An Domhain. All these are present there in abundance[8]!

The positive characteristics of An Domhain are rather fewer than for the Otherworld. They do, however, just as good a job of defining the essential nature of the place. They include an essential darkness, the grotesque, magical power, and the presence of constant conflict. The darkness or shadows of An Domhain are proverbial. It is sometimes called the land of Scáth (shadow). The darkness of the depths of the sea are as important to the definition of An Domhain as their cold. Often, the creatures of An Domhain can only come forth by night, or only on Samhain Eve, and are banished by the light. The grotesque may be even more prevalent than darkness in An Domhain. Fortresses are made of bones[9]. Headless bodies and bodiless heads are common, and not necessarily dead[10]. Three-headed giants lay waste to the land[11]. Flocks of birds whither up whatever they breathe upon[12]. There is a prevalence of the bizarre, the ugly, and the threatening. On the other hand, the Fomoire themselves are very powerful, magically, and the Gods learn various types of magical art in An Domhain, often in order to use those arts against their Fomorian inventors. As one might expect, these are mostly forms of **mallacht,** or cursing. From here, for example, Lugh learned the **corrguinacht**, the art of encircling his enemies on one foot, with one eye closed, and one arm extended, which he then used to defeat the Fomoire at Mag Tuired[13]. The presence of constant conflict is also mentioned in many descriptions of An Domhain. Indeed, it is from An Domhain that many of the most potent arts of the warrior come. It is most probably there, for example, that Cúchulainn goes to complete his warrior training, and in many accounts, the wars of its kings are mentioned[14]. Crom Dubh is not a king without opposition, though there is no reason to regard his opponents as being any better than he. In addition, the ferocity and destructiveness of almost every being that enters this world from An Domhain is notable. We have mentioned three headed giants, but perhaps we should also mention boars, bulls, and ferocious cats that come from An Domhain in various tales to wreak havoc on the Earth[15].

**The Fomoire and the Tuatha Dé Danann:** The Fomoire and the Tuatha Dé Danann are enemies. This is a constant conflict, the background to all our myths, and an essential aspect of the theology of my version of Irish Paganism. The cosmic war represents my "default", and in my opinion the most traditional, view of the "Problem of Evil" and of theodicy. Despite the conflict, neither Fomoire nor Tuatha Dé Danann are pure abstractions, or perfect. As I have already mentioned, they are real, imperfect beings, capable of making mistakes, having passions, and so on. This also applies to the Fomoire, who are not all necessarily beyond the possibility of redemption. Though it is very rare, it is known for Fomoire to have been born with a nature more suited to life among the Tuatha Dé Danann, and to have joined the people among whom they actually belong. Likewise, a few rare Fomoire have overcome their nature, and have adopted the ideology of Fírinne, thus "defecting" to the side of the Tuatha Dé Danann. Finally, various marriages and less licit sexual encounters have produced children of mixed parentage, who eventually chose one side or the other. So, we see that the two sides are not watertight or absolute.

Despite the above, the general rule is still that the Tuatha Dé Danann and Fomoire are at war, and that it is a war to the finish. That being the case, who will win? Whom should we bet on? Well, the Tuatha Dé Danann create ordered societies, in which beings cooperate, and work together for the greater good. They generally bring prosperity and other benefits to those who worship them. They have many allies outside their own community. The Fomoire, by contrast, exist in a perpetual state of conflict, and work together only grudgingly, under duress. They waste vast energies on pointless internal feuds and betrayals. They likewise betray and oppress those foolish enough to worship them, leading them to have few followers, indeed. They have likewise few allies or friends. They are not trusted, even by one another.

In consequence, we can say that the Tuatha Dé Danann are winning. They have been for millions or even billions of years. It is a very slow, grinding process, taking place on a cosmic scale. Still, it does take place. Though the Fomoire do gain the upper hand here and there, sometimes for centuries or millennia at a time, the Gods eventually drive them back, and then back again. Eventually, the Gods will win, and all that is evil and unpleasant will be destroyed. Those Fomoire who can be recovered or rehabilitated will be. The others, and Crom Dubh, will perish forever. Then, this world will be like the Otherworld in its pleasures and beauties.

Do not expect it right away, however. There is very little in the old traditions that would lead us to expect an Armageddon, or any change in the basic nature of the universe. It will be a battleground, a middle place, for many, many thousands or millions of years yet to come. We can, however, help the Gods win locally, on our own Earth, in our societies, institutions and towns. We can do this by living according to Fírinne, by practicing Íobairt, by doing what we can to advance the cause of Truth and Right. In this small, human way, we can help to improve our own lives, improve our society, and even, in a small way, bring the final victory of the Gods that much closer.

**Protection Against the Fomoire:** A lot of ink has been spilled, and a lot of trees have died discussing the issue of "psychic self defense". Now, in my own opinion, after more than 20 years of practice in various occult communities, such things as "shields" and "wards", and so on are usually ineffective, and not often needed. Much more often than not, bad fortune or the belief that one is being "psychically attacked" are the result of one's own bad decisions and delusions. Every now and then, however, though very rarely, there are cases of real mallacht or actual Fomorian presence. Luckily for such cases, the old lore includes plenty of remedies that work about as well today as they did long ago.

How, then can one defend against Fomorian influence? Probably the best single substance for protecting against Fomorian influence, and against other forms of mallacht, is rowan wood. The wood of the European rowan, or, to a much lesser extent its North American cousin, has long been noted in the lore to drive out Fomors and other unpleasant spiritual beings. A stick or even splinter of rowan wood will usually suffice. For whatever reason, the Fomoire appear to hate the color red, and so red thread has also been used against them. Indeed, red thread can be enchanted with a protective incantation to increase its strength, or wrapped about a sprig of rowan for even greater protective power[16].

If these are not available, then other means may be used. Holy water, of any type, including Christian holy water, in my experience, will usually drive the lesser Fomoire away forthwith[17]. Likewise, the light of any kind of sacred fire, from any tradition, again, is a strong barrier to them, and greatly reduces their ability to cause mischief. They also dislike ordinary light, and will avoid it unless fairly determined. In this regard, sunlight is more effective than electric light, which is better than nothing, but not much[18]. Salt is well known in many traditions as a protective, and it is no different in Gaelic tradition. Salt can be used to hallow and protect places, and greatly impedes the work of the Fomoire[19].

Cold Iron is spoken of often, but it is not always clear what is meant, nor if it really works. I have never known ordinary steel to have protective properties. On the other hand, I know people who swear by nails made from pure iron, not steel, so perhaps there is something to this[20]. Many traditions, mostly promoted by the Church, speak of the effectiveness of Christian rites and prayers, notably church bells[21]. These same traditions usually speak of the evil spirits that may come to inhabit churches, so perhaps we should take them with a grain of salt. I have, certainly, never known Christian rites to be more effective than any others.

## Types of Fomors

This list is not meant to be comprehensive. It is, instead, a list of typical sorts of Fomorian spirit, which can give some idea of the various types of nastiness out there. Note that most Fomoire are exceedingly rare, though some of the least powerful of them are merely very uncommon.

**Bogies:** A class of minor spirit whose primary joy is in tormenting others. They are said to be skilled shape-shifters, but most often appear as small, troll-like beings of great ugliness. Bogies are said to enjoy causing bad luck, and luring people to cliffs and other dangerous places. Very rarely, a bogy will pick a particular person to follow about for years, sending illness and misfortune to them. Although a few bogies live in groups, the vast majority are solitary spirits[22].

**Brollachan:** The brollachan is a shapeless, nearly mindless creature, which is believed to inhabit certain remote forests and swamps. It delights in engulfing travelers and frightening them, though it can actually do little or no harm. It has a cold, slimy feel, a foul smell, and looks like a coherent fog-bank. A few brollachans are companions of a more dangerous fuath, or water spirit, but most are solitary beings. It is entirely possible that the brollachan is merely a poetic description of the fog produced by rotting swamp vegetation, which is often rich in methane gas[23].

**Fachan:** The word fachan is a later, Scottish term for the most dangerous and powerful of the Fomoire. These beings are the primary opponents of the Gods in ancient myth, with a few exercising almost God-like power[24]. While a very few of them have sometimes concerned themselves with human beings, most are occupied with fighting against the Gods, hoping someday to enslave all the world. The sort of misfortune they usually send is directed against the entire community, a disaster such as an epidemic or famine. Here is a description of this type of Fomor from an ancient Irish manuscript:

> ......this is how he was: he held a very thick iron flail-club in his skinny hand, and twenty chains out of it, and fifty apples on each chain of them, and a venomous spell on each apple of them..... and one eye in the forehead of his black-faced countenance, and one bare, hard, very hairy arm coming out of his chest, and one veiny, thick soled leg supporting him......[25]

**Fuath:** Fuathan are a class of very evil and dangerous water spirits. They are said to come in a wide variety of forms, few of which are even vaguely humanoid. Some delight in wrecking the affairs and farms of rural communities: blighting crops, sending diseases, and killing people traveling alone at night. More commonly, they only attack those who go into the water. Luckily, they are believed to be even more exceedingly rare than the common run of Fomor, generally inhabiting remote bodies of water, and avoiding inhabited regions. They are invariably solitary spirits. The Each-Uisge, the "water horse" of Highland mythology is a very special type of Fuath, which takes equine and human form[26]. Note the resemblance between Fuathan and various types of lake and sea serpents reported even to this day.

**Sluagh:** The sluagh, the name means merely "host" or "crowd", are a swarm of particularly horrid aerial spirits. Some say that they are the spirits of the evil dead, rejected by the Earth and the Otherworld alike. Be that as it may, they wander the upper air, fighting battles among themselves, and tormenting human beings and animals. They are said to be short and dark in appearance, often with stunted bodies and large heads. They are particularly fond of attacking travelers and cattle[27]. I will try to avoid making too many comparisons between the sluagh and those favorites of paranoid American folklore, the UFOs and mysterious cattle mutilators.............

# 6

# Íobairt: Sacrifice and Ritual

**The Essentials:** Fírinne includes not only an ethical system, a way of life, and the proper organization of human society, but also the proper way of worshipping the Tuatha Dé Danann. Indeed, the giving of worship in the proper way is a very important part of Fírinne. When human beings first came into the world, they agreed to give worship to the Gods, who in turn would give to them the fruits of nature. We have, all of us, been bound by this covenant ever since. The Tuatha Dé Danann are the true source of all that we have, and we in turn owe to them both that we shall care properly for the Earth, and that we shall show our gratitude and respect through the rituals of worship.

Worship and sacrifice in the old Gaelic tradition is called **Íobairt1.** The term actually refers to "giving to", or offering of items, with the implication of giving the render due from clients to their lords. In metaphysical terms, it is a way of showing respect for the Déithe, and so keeping human life in line with the cycles of the year, of life, and of nature. It includes the proper tools and places of worship, the proper method of ritual, a variety of daily prayers, a round of seasonal holidays, and several rites marking the stages of life. Together, these ingredients form the sacred setting and framework of Gaelic life.

**Places of Worship:** There are really two proper settings for Gaelic worship. The first is the home hearth or altar. This can be a very simple affair, as simple as the domestic hearth in any culture. In houses that have them, the fireplace is the logical place for this. All that is needed is to place a **Dealbh**, an image of a divinity on the mantle, and any tools you wish to use before the fire. Offerings, which should be flammable or at least not damaging to the fire, can be poured directly into the flames, or else set into the coals. In cases where the offering is not burnable, then it should be passed through the fire and into an offering bowl, which can be set outside, or into a lake, river, or stream.

The next traditional setting for Gaelic worship is the **Neimheadh**[2], the sanctuary, the holy place. Neimhidh are usually out of doors, but in these times, that rule no longer is universal. In general terms, a Neimheadh is very simple, just a space, usually but not always square, set aside for sacred purposes. In practice, owing to the practical ingredients of Íobairt itself, a Neimheadh has the following elements:

## I. An Neimheadh – The Ancient Celtic Temple Space:

### A.    An Teorainn (uh tor-oin), the boundary:
1. Description: Ancient Celtic temples were marked out by a boundary, usually a ditch and embankment. Often they were very shallow, no more than a foot or so high, and so clearly symbolic. Other times, they were larger – genuine fortifications. Other forms of boundary have survived from other, related cultures, including wooden fences, stone walls, colonnades, and even simple threads marking the sacred space. Most such boundaries were square, but a very few were round. We do not know why.
2. Function: The teorainn marks out the sacred space from the mundane world. It symbolizes the idircheo, the barriers between this world and the Other, as well as the boundary between the ordered world of human society and the chaotic outside.
3. Sources: Archaeology. The vast majority of Celtic temples which have been excavated have such boundaries, perhaps all of them[3].

### B.    An Teallach (uh tyell-ach), the Hearth:
1. Description: The vast majority of ancient temples had a hearth in or near the center of the space. These were simple fire pits, and could be of almost any size or description.
2. Function: The hearth was the center of the sacred space, where burned the sacred fire representing divine power and light. The sacred fire could itself receive prayers and sacrifices, and also served to purify and protect the sacred space. In both early and modern

Gaelic folk-custom, the hearth is the center of the home, where most of the domestic prayers are said, and rituals performed.

3. Sources: Archaeology, and also modern Irish and Scots folk-custom, as well as the customs of other Indo-European peoples, including the Romans, Greeks, Baltic peoples, Slavs, and Hindus, among others4.

**C. An Tobar (uh taw-bur), the Well:**
1. Description: Many, but not all, old temples had ritual shafts into which offerings could be put. A few were located near rivers, lakes, or bogs which may have served the same purpose. Such shafts could be very deep, and a few had a skull, possibly of a slain enemy or a revered elder, at the very bottom. Basically, they were just really deep holes. In smaller temples, and modern reconstructions, an offering bowl must serve the same purpose.
2. Function: The well was the gateway to the Otherworld, and one of two ways that offerings could be sent to the Gods, the other being through the sacred fire. These wells need to be distinguished from the numerous holy wells scattered around Ireland, which were usually springs sacred to Goddesses. The wells attached to temples received offerings; sacred wells gave holy and often healing water.
3. Sources: Archaeology. Many such ritual shafts are known, and other offering pits are found in ancient temples5.

**D. An Dealbh (uh jel-ev), the Image:**
1. Description: Most old temples had images of the Gods worshipped there. While only a few such images have been recovered by archaeologists, most old temples have post holes near the offering wells, which probably served to hold sacred images which have since been lost. Usually, these images were deliberately constructed in a simple, even crude manner, simple posts with human figures and the symbols of one or another deity carved on them. This may have been to emphasize that images are purely symbolic of a mysterious spiritual essence, but we cannot be sure. Such thinking would have been in keeping with other aspects of ancient Celtic thought, however. Some images were simple standing stones, trees, or other objects of purely symbolic meaning. Even in the Iron Age, a few were more naturalistic statues in Greco-Roman style.
2. Function: An image was a symbol of a deity, and the temporary dwelling place of the deity when it was invoked. As such, they had an important ritual function, and were occasionally smeared with offerings.

3. Sources: For once, both the archaeology and Irish literature are in essential agreement. We have plenty of remains of statues of the Gods, and the Irish vernacular sources mention "idols" which were worshipped by early Irish Pagans[6].

**E.   An Bile (un beel-yuh), the World Tree:**
1. Description: A few temples had large pillars which stood in the temple space. They were not, apparently, part of any building. A few have been recovered, and some of them have been carved with leaves and the like. In the Rhineland, and in adjacent areas of modern France, we also find a type of monument called "Jupiter Giant Columns", which may shed light on these pillars. These are huge pillars with a monster, often with serpents for arms and legs at the bottom, and a horseman bearing a thunderbolt at the top. It is quite clear that they depict the world tree with a deity much like the Dagda or Lugh in the heavens and some kind of demon, perhaps similar to Balor, in the underworld. From this, one can deduce that the pillars found in temples similarly depicted the world tree.
2. Function: The bile symbolizes the world tree. It is not used in any known rituals, though maypole dancing may, or may not, be derived from some kind of similar ideas among the Germanic peoples.
3. Sources: Archaeology and what is known of ancient cosmology. It should be noted that such pillars are not known in Irish literature, nor do I know of any examples from Ireland[7].

Personal Tools and Sacred Items: The term for such tools is Cleathainsaí, a term which carries the sense of "paraphernalia, stuff, gear"[8]. The term is appropriate given how many different such items there are, and the general lack of consensus on their use. The following is merely a list of the most common tools used in the old literature, in folklore, and in modern practice, with some notes as to how they are used. It is fairly comprehensive, but there are bound to be differences in how various people perceive them and use them:

## II.  Cleathansaí – Ritual Gear and Tools:

**A.   An Claíomh (uh cleave), the Sword:**
1. Description: Just a sword, preferably of ancient Celtic design. A knife may be substituted, though it has its own symbolic meaning.

2. Function: The Sword is the symbol of battle, conflict, hardiness, victory, and the warrior nobility. It is one of the Four treasures of the Tuatha Dé Danann.
  3. Sources: Ancient Irish literature, especially Cath Mag Tuired, and the Settling of the Manor of Tara[8].

**B. An Coire (uh corra), the Cauldron:**
  1. Description: A large iron or brass cauldron. A chalice may be substituted.
  2. Function: The Cauldron symbolizes prosperity, fertility, abundance, and ordinary tribe members. It is used for rituals involving generosity and fertility. It is one of the Four Treasures of the Tuatha Dé Danann.
  3. Sources: As above[9].

**C. An Chraobh Cheoil (uh chroyv chyoil, with the "ch" like in German), the Musical Branch:**
  1. Description: A tree branch covered with bells, and other golden and silver decorations. A "druid's chain" consisting of a chain of bells and similar baubles may be substituted.
  2. Function: The Musical Branch symbolizes the Otherworldly, the mysterious, music, inspiration, and the outcasts of the tribe. It can be used as a rattle to induce altered states of consciousness.
  3. Sources: Early Irish literature, mostly the Táin, as well as the imram tales, and others[10].

**D. An tSleá (uh tlaw), the Spear:**
  1. Description: A spear, preferably of ancient Celtic design. A wand or spear-head may be substituted, though wands have their own symbolic meaning.
  2. Function: The Spear symbolizes knowledge, wisdom, the lightening, intellect, and the Aes Dána. It is one of the Four Treasures of the Tuatha Dé Danann.
  3. Sources: Ancient Irish literature, especially Cath Mag Tuired, and the Settling of the Manor of Tara[11].

**E. An Lia (uh lee-uh), the Stone:**
  1. Description: A large, flat stone, though other sorts of stones are used, and a small rock may be used for home altars.
  2. Function: The Stone symbolizes sovereignty, rulership, legitimacy, stability, primacy, and the rulers of the Tribe. It is used in the inauguration of the ruler, and is one of the Four Treasures of the Tuatha Dé Danann.
  3. Sources: As above[12].

F.  **An tScian (uh tskee-un), the Knife:**
   1. Description: A double-edged knife, a tiny bit like the traditional Wiccan athame. Other knives may be substituted.
   2. Function: A general tool, and the symbol of tribe membership and freedom. All free tribe members normally carried such a knife.
   3. Sources: Early and modern Scottish tradition, with some echoes in both early and modern Irish tradition[13].

G.  **An Brat (uh brawt), the Mantle:**
   1. Description: A nine yard rectangle of woolen cloth, usually about a yard in width. These are also the traditional dimensions of the Great Kilt of the Scottish Highlands, but the traditional Irish brat was worn about the body like a very large cloak.
   2. Function: The brat was a cloak, of course, but was also a symbol of tribe membership and rank. The length of the brat and the number of colors in it differed by rank.
   3. Sources: Early Irish literature and tradition[14].

H.  **An tSlat (uh tlawt), the Wand:**
   1. Description: A straight, wooden wand, stick, or staff. A wand may also be usable as a **bata**, a fighting stick.
   2. Function: Several. A wand was carried by anyone with rank as a Druid, poet, Seer, or ruler, though in the last case it had to be a peeled hazel wand. It was probably a focus for buachatheamh, as emphasized in many tales, and in the stereotype of the "magic wand".
   3. Sources: Many. The wand is mentioned in most of the ancient Irish tales, and shows up in more modern folklore, as well[15].

I.  **An Mhuince (uh voo-ink-uh), the Torc:**
   1. Description: The Celtic neck-ring, usually thick, of gold, silver or bronze, and worn about the neck.
   2. Function: A symbol of rank, and also of being bound to the Gods.
   3. Sources: Universal in Celtic art and clothing[16].

J.  **An Chorr Bholg (uh corr voll-eg), the Crane Bag:**
   1. Description: A bag, possibly of crane skin. The original Corr Bolg was larger on the inside than on the outside. This is hard to do nowadays.
   2. Function: To keep sacred stuff in. Possibly serves as a sort of Gaelic "medicine bag", though there is no evidence of this.
   3. Sources: Various stories of Manannán mac Lir, ancient and modern[17].

Methods of Íobairt: Our knowledge of the ancient rituals and methods of worship is based primarily on the surviving rituals and folk-customs of the modern Celtic peoples, who have preserved much that is genuinely ancient, often under the thinnest of Christian veneers.  In addition, we have a good knowledge from the ancient texts of the words used for various religious practices, which allow us to reconstruct the old worship techniques with a high degree of accuracy.  Together, these along with comparative knowledge from related traditions and some measure of inspiration, allow us to worship in the proper manner, and to keep the covenant made by our spiritual ancestors.

**Daily Prayers:**  Probably the most important form of worship in the lives of the modern Celtic peoples are the daily prayers, which traditionally have been used to sanctify almost every activity throughout the day.  Although the modern Gaels mostly consider themselves Christians, these folk-prayers are often of clearly Pagan origin, calling upon and praising the old Gods and heroes, or the elements of nature.  There are literally thousands of such prayers, for every type of work and household activity.  Many of them are recognized by modern scholars as among the great monuments of Gaelic, and world, folk-poetry, moving works in the own right, even separated from what they tell us of early Gaelic religion.  To learn more of them, I recommend Alexander Carmichael's *Carmina Gadelica*, a collection made in the Scottish Highlands in the 19th Century.  A few samples are below, all adapted to a purely Pagan idiom, and all prayers that would have been heard throughout the day in ancient times.  Somewhat unusually for this book, I have left these prayers in Scots Gaelic, rather than Irish.  I am not quite up to the task of translating from Scots to Irish without creating something that does insult to both languages.

## III. Urnaithe – Prayers:

A.  **Sun Greeting**[18] **To be said to the sun as it rises, at dawn, in praise of Áine.**

<u>A' Ghrian</u>

Fàilte ort féin, a ghrian na'n tràth,
'S tu siùbhal ard nan speur;
Do cheummaibh treun air scéith nan ard,
'S tu màthair àigh nan reul.

Tu laighe sìos an cuan na dìth,
Gun dìobhaill is gun scàth;
Thu 'g éirigh suas air stuagh na sìth,
Ma rioghan óg ina bhláth.

## The Sun

Greetings to you, sun of the season
And you walking high in the heavens
Your steps strong on the wings of the heights
And you the glorious mother of the stars.

It is you lying down in the harbor of danger (ie. the sea)
Without bedevilment and without dread;
It is you rising up on the peaked wave of peace
Like a young queen in flower.

**B.     Moon Greeting[19] To be said to the moon, on its rising, in praise of Boann.**

## Rioghain na h-Oiche

Fàilte dhuit féin,
Éiteag na h-oidhche!

Àilleachd nan speur,
Éiteag na h-oidhche!

Màthair nan reul,
Éiteag na h-oidhche!

Dalta na gréine,
Éiteag na h-oidhche!

Mórachd nan reul,
Éiteag na h-oidhche!

## Queen of the Night

Welcome to yourself,
Gem of night!

Beauty of the heavens,
Gem of night!

Mother of the stars,
Gem of night!

Fosterling of the sun,
Gem of night!

Greatness of the stars,
Gem of night!

**C.    Night Shielding[20] To be said upon going to bed, in order to shield from harm**

<u>Urnaí chodla</u>

A mi cur m'anama 's mo chorp
Air do chomaraig, a Dhánann
Air do chomaraig, a Mhacha
Air do chomaraig a Mhórríghan na fírinne reidh
An Triur a sheasadh mo chuis,
Is nach cuireadh an cul rium fein.

Thus, a Dhánann, tha caomh agus ceart
Thus a Mhacha, cur an flaitheas na'n Tir
Thus a Mhórríghan tha lan nam bua
Da mo gleidheadh an nochd o thruaigh;
An Triur a dheanadh mo cheart
Mo gleidheadh an nochd 's gach uair.

<u>Sleep Prayer</u>

I am putting my soul and my body
On your sanctuary, o Dánann
On your sanctuary, o Macha
On your sanctuary, o Mórrígan of ready truth
The Trinity who would defend my cause
And not turn their backs upon me.

It is you, a Dánann, who art kind and right

It is you, o Macha, who gives the sovereignty of the Land
It is you, o Mórrígan, who art full of strength/victory/virtue
My protection this night from harm
The Trinity who would do me right
My protection tonight and always.

D.     **Meal Prayer**[21] To be said over a meal, as thanksgiving to the Gods who gave it, and to the beings who gave their lives to be part of it.

<u>Buíochas an Bheile</u>

Tang dhut a Dhagda
Moladh dhut a Dhagda
Urram dhut a Dhagda
An dhéidh na thug thu dhomh.

<u>Thanks of the Meal</u>

Thanks to you, o Dagda
Praise to you, o Dagda
Reverence to you, o Dagda
For all you have given to me.

    **The Ritual Outline:** The following ritual outline is designed to be rather minimal in its essence, performing just the functions needed to frame an Íobairt to any particular deity. It must be pointed out that true Gaelic ritual is almost never complex, but rather is simple and filled with meaning for the community as a whole. Holidays, for example, would include communal activities and celebrations, but not elaborate ceremonies. Still, it is necessary, especially today, to mark out the beginning and end of a solemn or sacred act, to bless the space in which sacred acts are to be performed, and to protect that space from desecration or impurity. When I make Íobairt myself, I do it in Irish, normally, but I recognize that most people reading this do not likely speak the language, and so have prepared this English version.

    I.     **Íonú/Purification:** This is designed to cleanse the participants of any lingering negative emotions and energies left behind by everyday life, before beginning the ritual. Normally, this is done by taking a pitcher, bowl and towels around the group, and allowing everyone present to wash his or her hands. When this is done, the water in the bowl is poured outside the circle, and something said to the effect of: "I cast from this holy place all impurities and impediments of the spiritual and material worlds".

II. **Beannacht na'n Neimheadh/Blessing of the Neimheadh:** This is how sacred space is made. It establishes ritual space, and serves as an introduction to the ritual, as well as establishing a protective circle around the holy space.

    A. **Déanamh na'n Thine Cnáimhe/Making the Sacred Fire:** This creates the sacred fire, which represents divinity in unmanifest form, and also serves as a gateway to the divine realm. In addition, the light of the Sacred Fire is a powerful protective force. Light the fire candle, and say:

> You are the center of creation
> The first fire, at the beginning of time.
> You are the light of the sun
> Which marks out day from night.
> You are the fire of every hearth,
> All fires are lit from you.
> You are the light of the Goddess,
> Which dwells in all of us.
> I raise you fire, in the way of Brigid
> Here on the holy hearth

    B. **Déanamh na'n Uisce Naofa/Making of the Holy Water:** This creates holy water, which symbolize the motherhood and love of Dánu. They are also used in certain rituals, notably in rituals against the Evil Eye. Place your finger or the tip of your knife in the water, visualize a green-blue light filling it, and the power of Dánu in the light. Say:

> You are the Mother of the Gods,
> The Source of All Life.
> You are the Source of all wisdom,
> The keeper of all secrets.
> You are the source of all love,
> Who nourishes the world.
> You are the Lady of the Land,
> Source of all Sovereignty.
> Without you, we are nothing;
> With you we are made whole.

**Déanamh na'n Airbhe/Making the Hedge:** This establishes the protective and sanctifying hedge of power about the neimheadh. Light a small candle from the Hearth Candle, take it about the neimheadh, visualizing its light forming a thick, tall, protective barrier about the holy space.

III. **Íobairt féin/Offering Proper:** This is the actual offering to the deity of the ritual, and the recitation of prayers and incantations. The deity is invoked. Then power is given to the deity, and allegiance shown him or her in the form of an offering. This causes power to be returned by the deity, which is then bound using a spell, or used in a seasonal drama, or some other ritual.

- A. **Achainí/Invocation:** This is the invocation of the deity. There are many of them, each unique. See Appendix B for a good collection.
- B. **Dícheadal/Incantation or Urnai/Prayer:** Here, the blessing of the deity is sought, and the energy coming from the deity used in its proper way.

## IV  Deireadh na'n Íobairt

- A. **Slánú na'n Uisce Naofa/Saving the Holy Water:** This is the opposite of the making of the Waters of Life, and is designed to "save" the energy of the Waters of Life in the bodies of the participants. Say:

    You are the Mother of the Gods
    The source of all life.
    You are the source of all wisdom,
    The keeper of all secrets.
    You are the source of all love,
    Who nourishes the world.
    You are the Lady of the Land,
    The source of all sovereignty.
    We take you into ourselves,
    That we be made whole.

Now, drink the water, or pass the cup around to all participants.

- B. **Smúrchoigilt na'n Thine Cnáimhe/Saving the Sacred Fire:** This is the opposite of Making the Sacred Fire. The Sacred Fire is saved in the hearth candle, or hearth generally, from which the energy can be called for later rituals. Visualize the energy of the fire sinking into the candle, and becoming a dull but persistent and warm glow which will not go out. Say:

    You are the center of creation,

The first fire, at the beginning of time.
You are the light of the sun,
Which marks out day from night.
You are the fire of every hearth,
All fires are lit from you.
You are the light of the Goddess,
Which dwells in all of us.
I save you, fire, as Brigid would save you
Inside the holy hearth.

   C.   **An Deireadh/Final Closing:** Blow out the fire candle, and say:

> Ta an íobairt deanta
> Daoine 's déithe
> Dulaige muide as an Neimheadh
> Neartach 's lan
> Le gra in ár gcroithe.
>
> The offering is made, the rite complete.
> Let us go from this place made whole,
> And filled with love for one another.
> That's it,
> It is completed.

**An Bhliain, The Year:** Time, in the ancient Gaelic worldview is created by the alternation of the great cosmic principles which correspond to light and darkness, summer and winter. Likewise, the year is seen as a recapitulation of both the entire history of the cosmos and the individual life cycle. In this, the Gaelic year is not wholly dissimilar in principle from the Wiccan year, though the exact symbolism, and the rites with which the year are celebrated have a quite different character. The **feilte,** the great seasonal holidays, mark the turning of this mighty cycle, the changes from one season to another, and the peaks of these seasons. They also mark different points in the cycle whereby bua moves through the landscape. To celebrate these holidays, then, is to align oneself with those forces, and to participate to that extent in the cycle that is a part of Fírinne. The actual holidays, their meanings, and some of the rites traditionally associated with them are as follows:

# I. Samhain:

A. **Description:** Samhain (sow-unn) marks the beginning of the Gaelic Year, and the year's holiest day. It is also the transition from the Light Half of the year to the Dark Half, and from Autumn to Winter. It is thus a night between one year and another, one season and another. For this reason, it is considered a time of awesome portent, outside of normal time and the normal order of nature, when the Idircheo, the barriers between the worlds, are down, and spirits and people can move freely and even accidentally from one world to another.

B. **Date:** For three nights – variously from October 31 to November 2, or around November 7, or around the new moon nearest these dates.

C. **Meaning of Name:** Summer's End

D. **The Samhain Ritual:**
   1. **The Neimheadh:** For Samhain, the Neimheadh should be decorated with dark colors, mostly what used to called Earth tones – black, brown, dark green, dark gold, midnight blue, dark red. Candles should also be in such colors. Decorations can includes sheaves of grain, autumn leaves, gourds, pumpkins, jack o' lanterns, and photos of deceased ancestors and relatives. Typical American Halloween decorations – black cats, witches, skeletons, horror movie characters, and the like – are *not* appropriate. A number of unlit candles should be distributed about the space. The attendees should be dressed in dark colors, and masked, but not actually in costume. Masks may be made by hand (there are a number of good books on the subject), or purchased from appropriate vendors. Deep enough hoods, pulled so as to hide the face, are also appropriate as a substitute.
   2. **Íonú/Purification:** This should be done as in the Ritual Outline.
   3. **Beannacht na'n Neimheadh/Blessing of the Neimheadh:** As per the ritual outline.
   4. **Íobairt Fein/Offering Proper:**
      a. Aichaini/Invocation:
         To the Mórríghan:
         Great Mórríghan
         Lady of Fate
         Lady of Prophecy
         Lady of the Night
         Come tonight!
      Victorious Mórrígan
      Queen of Battles

Queen of Frenzies
Queen of Ravens
Come tonight!

Come to our neimheadh
Where we are giving you honor!

To the Ancestors:
Ancestors
Fathers of our Flesh
Mothers of our Blood
Heroes of Old
Come tonight!

Ancestors
Grandfathers and Grandmothers
Who inspire us
Who teach us
Who watch over us
Come tonight!

Come to our Neimheadh
Where we are giving you honor!

To the Land Spirits:
People of Peace
Dwellers in the Mounds
Dwellers in the Land
Dwellers in the Forest
Come tonight!

People of Peace
Who give abundance
Who give luck
Who give strange wisdom
Come tonight!

Come to our Neimheadh
Where we are giving you honor!

b. The New Fire: Light a small candle from the hearth candle and go about the sacred space, lighting all of the candles that have

been distributed about the space for this purpose. As you do so, say:
Ta solas ag teacht o'n dorchadas
Ta tine nua ag loscadh air gach Teallach
Ta blain nua ag tosú air an oiche naofa seo.
(English version)
Light is coming from the darkness
A new fire is burning on every hearth
A new year is beginning on this holy night.

5. **Deireadh na'n Íobairt/Closing:** as per ritual outline
6. **Feast:** The feast should be a dumb supper with additional three places set – one each for the Mórrígan, the Ancestors, and the Daoine Sídhe. Afterward, seasonal divination games may take place, along with storytelling, music, and dancing.

## II. Imbolc:

A. **Description:** The festival of Imbolc (immulk) marks the beginning of the Spring Quarter of the year, the Light Half of the Dark Half of the Year. The power of life now moves from the Otherworld up into the Land, and begins to quicken. This small, seemingly insignificant force, yet so full of promise is often symbolized by a serpent which comes from a burial mound, but even more often by the Brigid Óg, the Young Brigid, who is adored on this day. Imbolc is above all the festival of Brigid, both as the young year and as a mother. It is also a festival of youth, of girls and boys, and of the home and hearth. All of these, of course, celebrate life, fertility, and promise, the promise which is now developing.

B. **Date:** February 1-2, or sometime around February 7, or the New Moon closest to those dates.

C. **Meaning of Name:** Unknown. May be derived from Old Celtic terms meaning "purification", or "Ewe's Milk".

D. **The Imbolc Ritual:**
   1. **The Neimheadh:** For Imbolc, the Neimheadh should be decorated in white, with occasional flashes of red. It must be meticulously clean. Candles should all be white. A cloth baby doll in a cradle should be placed on the altar. This is the **Brigid Óg,** which represents the Goddess Brigid as a young child, and thus symbolizes the power of life, as well. There should be a peeled wooden wand, preferably of hazel wood, on one side of the altar.

Brigid's Wheels and Brigid's Crosses should be placed about the sacred space. The attendees should wear at least one white garment. Also, they should bring with them a small offering for Brigid. It need not be anything remotely fancy – a stone, a leaf, a coin, such things will do very well. Before the ritual the attendees should help make the Brigid's Wheels for the Neimheadh.

2. **Íonú/Purification:** as per ritual outline.
3. **Beannacht na'n Neimheadh/Blessing of the Neimheadh:** as per ritual outline
4. **Íobairt Fein/Offering Proper:**

   a. Aichaini/Invocation:

   Holy Brigid
   Goddess of the Hearth
   Goddess of Fire
   Goddess most excellent
   Come tonight!

   Goddess Brigid
   Lady of Poetry
   Lady of Smithcraft
   Lady of Healing
   Come tonight!
   Come to our Neimheadh
   Where we are giving you honor!

   b. Dícheadal/Incantation

   On the morning of the Feast Day of Brigid
   The Serpent shall come from the mound
   I shall not molest the Serpent
   Nor shall the Serpent molest me.

   The Genealogy of the Holy Goddess Brigid
   Radiant Flame of Gold, noble foster mother of fire
   Brigid, the daughter of Dugall the Brown
   Son of Áedh, son of Art, son of Conn
   Son of Crearar, son of Cis, son of Carmac, son of Carruin.

> Every day and every night
> That I say the Genealogy of Brigid
> I shall not be killed, I shall not be harried
> I shall not be put in cell, I shall not be wounded,
> Neither shall the Gods leave me in forgetfulness
>
> No fire, no sun, no moon shall burn me,
> No lake, no water, no sea shall drown me,
> No arrow of spirit nor dart of demon shall wound me
> And I under the protection of the Gods of Worship,
> And my gentle foster mother is my beloved Brigid.22

    c.    Adoration of Brigid: First the peeled wand should be presented to the Brigid Óg, by the highest ranking or oldest person present. Then all attendees should bring their offerings forward and set them reverently before the Brigid Óg.

1. **Deireadh na'n Íobairt/Closing:** as per the ritual outline
2. **Feast:** The Feast should be held on a table covered with a white tablecloth, with the best china and silverware available to the group. The Brigid Óg should be brought to the table and a place set for her. Dairy foods should be prominent in the menu.

### III.    Bealtaine:
  A.  **Description:** Bealtaine (bel-tuh-nuh) is in most respects the mirror of Samhain. The second holiest day of the year, it marks the transition from the Dark Half to the Light Half of the Year, and from Spring to Summer. Like Samhain, but to a lesser extent, it is a night when the Idircheo is down, and spirits are free to walk in this world, in this case because it is a night between one half of the year and the other. Like Samhain, it is a time when the usual laws of nature are in abeyance. In the case of Bealtaine, however this takes the form of trickery and pranks more than of awesome portent. The rules of hospitality are suspended, for to give away food or, especially, milk, on Bealtaine eve is to give away the luck of the house. The rules of sexuality are also to some extent suspended, so that Bealtaine is associated with elopements, illicit affairs, and even wild orgies. Because of this, Bealtaine is considered a very unlucky time to marry.

  B.  **Date:** May 1-2, or May 7-8, or the new moon nearest.
  C.  **Meaning of Name:** "Fires of Bel", or else "Bright Fire". I tend to favor "Bright Fire", because we have no known Bel in Irish mythol-

ogy, and nothing in surviving Gaulish tradition which would associate Belinus with this holiday. Beltaine is also called Cetsamhain, meaning "anti-Samhain", referring to its being opposite Samhain in the yearly cycle.

D. **The Bealtaine Ritual:**
1. **The Neimheadh** The Neimheadh should be decorated in bright, cheerful colors for Bealtaine. Candles should likewise be brightly colored. Decor should include lots of flowers, and perhaps a May-bush – a short bush decorated with bright ribbons, flowers, and crafts. The attendees should likewise be dressed in bright clothing, and garlands are always appropriate for Bealtaine.
2. **Íonú/Purification** – as per ritual outline
3. **Beannacht na'n Neimheadh/Blessing of the Neimheadh** – as per ritual outline
4. **Íobairt Fein/Offering Proper**
    a. Achainí/Invocation

    To Dánu

    Mother Dánu
    Mother of the Gods
    Mother of the Well
    Mother of Nurturing
    Come tonight!

    Mother Dánu
    Giver of Wisdom
    Giver of Prosperity
    Giver of Life
    Come Tonight!

    Come to our Neimheadh,
    Where we are giving you honor!

    To the Land Spirits – as per Samhain ritual

    b. Dícheadal – The Bealtaine Blessing

    Dánu, thou Mother of the Gods,
    Bless our flocks and our bearing kine;

Hate nor scathe let not come near us,
Drive from us the works of the wicked.

Keep thine eye every Monday and Tuesday
On the bearing kine and the pairing queys;
Accompany us from hill to sea,
Gather thyself the sheep and their progeny.

Every Wednesday and Thursday be with them,
Be thy gracious hand always about them;
Tend the cows down to their stalls,
Tend the sheep down to their folds.

Every Friday be thou, O Goddess, at their head,
Lead the sheep from the face of the hills;
With their little lambs following them,
Encompass them with the Gods' encompassing.

Every Saturday be likewise with them,
Bring the goats in with their young,
Every kid and goat to the seaside,
And from the peak of the mountain on high,
With cresses green about its summit.

The strength of the Gods be our shield in distress,
The strength of Lugh, his spear and his sling,
The strength of Dian Cécht, Physician of Health,
And of the Dagda Mór, Father of All.

And of (earlamh)
And of (earlamh)
And of every other spirit who protects us,
Who have earned our trust by heroic deeds.

Bless ourselves and our children,
Bless every one that shall come from our loins,
Bless him whose name we bear,
And bless her whose womb bore us.

Every holiness blessing and power,
Be yielded to us every time and every hour,

>    In the names of the holy Gods
>    And of the spirits and ancestors we revere.
>
>    Be the Host of the Gods to shield us downward,
>    Be the Host of the Gods to shield us upward,
>    Be the Host of the Gods to shield us roundward,
>    Accepting our Bealtaine blessing from us
>    Accepting our Bealtaine blessing from us.23

1. **Deireadh na'n Íobairt/Closing** – as per ritual outline
2. **Feast** – The Beltaine Feast should be a riotous affair, more party than feast. Loud music, drinking, dancing, all are part of the holiday. Think St. Patrick's Day for Pagans, but without schlocky shamrocks, leprechauns, and green beer.

## IV. Lughnasadh:

A. **Description:** Lughnasadh (Loo-na-saah) is preeminently the festival of Lugh, though it also marks the beginning of the Autumn, the Dark Half of the Light Half of the Year, and the beginning of the harvest. The forces of life have by Lughnasadh taken physical form in the crops, which must now be harvested. In Ireland, the harvest is presaged by the coming of late-summer thunderstorms, which then mark a cooling in the temperature. This kills the molds and fungi which would otherwise blight the crops of barley and wheat, and makes the heavy labor of the harvest go more easily and rapidly. In consequence, we can say that Lugh is present both in the weather and the labor of the harvesters, who work together to win the harvest for the Tribe from the forces of dissolution and destruction. This is symbolized in the myth of the triumph of Lugh over Balor, which thus becomes central to the festival itself. In addition, the fact of the harvest leads to the holding of harvest fairs at this time of year, both to celebrate and to pool labor. From this has grown the custom of holding the most important meeting of the Tribal Assembly at or about Lughnasadh.
B. **Date:** August 1, or about August 7, or the new moon nearest, with fairs and assemblies continuing for up to two weeks after.
C. **Meaning of Name:** "Feast of Lugh", from an old word meaning feast.
D. **The Lughnasadh Ritual:**

1. **The Neimheadh** – It is best to hold this festival out-of-doors, on a high place, maybe a hill. Failing that, the Neimheadh should be decorated in harvest colors – gold, tan, off-white, brown. Candles should likewise be gold, tan, or brown. Decor can include sheaves of grain, farm implements, gourds, apples, and so on. A simple figure (I once used a saw horse set on its side with a bucket for a head) of Balor should be set up on the South side of the Neimheadh. This figure should be deliberately rickety, so that it can be knocked down with ease by a thrown spear or missile. The attendees should wear practical, seasonal clothing, particularly if the ritual is held out of doors. Don't forget your insect repellant!
2. **Íonú/Purification** – as per the ritual outline
3. **Beannacht na'n Neimheadh/Blessing of the Neimheadh** – as per ritual outline
4. **Íobairt Fein/Offering Proper**
    a. Achainí/Invocation

    Lord Lugh
    Lugh Lamhfhada
    Lugh Samildánach
    Lugh, Slayer of Balor
    Come tonight!

    Lord Lugh
    God of Lightning
    God who gives the Harvest
    God with the Spear
    Come tonight!

    Come to our Neimheadh
    Where we are giving you honor!

    b. Reenactment of the Slaying of Balor – one of the attendees takes a spear or ball symbolizing the tathlum, both of which are known in different versions of the story as the weapon Lugh used against Balor, and throws it at the "Balor" figure, hopefully knocking it apart. Everyone cheers.

    c. Lugh the Victorious

Thou Lugh the Victorious,
I make my circuit under thy shield,
Thou Lugh of the Shining Spear,
And of the brilliant blades,
Conqueror of the Dragon
Be thou at my back,
Thou ranger of the heavens,
Thou warrior and King of the Gods,
    O Lugh the Victorious,
    My pride and my guide,
    O Lugh the Victorious,
    The glory of mine eye.

I make my circuit,
In the friendship of the God,
On the machair, on the meadow,
On the cold, heathery hill;
Though I should travel ocean,
And the hard globe of the world,
No harm can ever befall me,
'Neath the shelter of thy shield,
    O Lugh the Victorious,
    Jewel of my heart,
    O Lugh the Victorious,
    The World's protector thou art.

Be the Sacred Host of the Gods,
Aye at peace with us,
With our horses, with our cattle,
With our wooly sheep in flocks,
With the crops growing in the field
Or ripening in the sheaf,
On the machair, on the moor,
In cole, in heap, or stack,
    Every thing on high low,
    Every furnishing and flock,
    Belongs to the Holy Host of the Gods,
    And to Lugh the Victorious.[24]

    d.    The Offering of Flowers – flowers are placed silently into a tobar, symbolizing the end of summer, and beginning of the harvest season. It is also very acceptable to offer them to Dánu.

1. **Deireadh na'n Íobairt/Closing** – as per Ritual Outline
2. **Feast** – The Feast should feature lots of grains – breads, vegetable and meat pies, various cooked grains, muffins, cakes or cookies for desert perhaps. Generally, the Lughnasadh Feast also features some revelry, mostly expressed as (traditional) music and dancing. It is customary for couples to leap together over the fire at Lughnasadh, as a form of magic for fertility and/or prosperity. It is also customary to have various athletic and other contests at Lughnasadh, usually before the ritual. In the days after the feast, the group should hold its annual meeting, select officers, resolve disputes, and generally reaffirm the social order.

# 7

# Death, and the Dead

That the spirits of the dead live on in the Otherworld is an aspect of Irish Pagan tradition that has never disappeared. The Greco-Roman authors wrote much on the Celtic belief in a life after death, indicating that the belief in a post-mortem realm having characteristics much like those of Tír na'n Óg was a regular feature of ancient Gaulish belief. According to Pomponius Mela, the best known doctrine of the Druids was that "soul are eternal, and there is another life in the infernal regions"1. Other sources describe Celts carrying the payment of debts into the next world2.

These beliefs are echoed in Irish folklore as late as the present day. Within the last 30 to 50 years, there have been people in Ireland who continued to believe, in flat contradiction of their Catholic faith, that the souls of the dead can be seen at night flying over the Skellig rocks on their way to the Land of the Young – that is, to the Otherworld of their Pagan ancestors3.

In early Irish belief the Lord of the Dead is Donn, brother of Éremón, the first king of the Milesians. Donn offended the Goddess Ériu, one of the Éarlaimh of all the land of Ireland, and then urged the slaughter of all the Tuatha Dé Danann should the Milesians gain final possession of Ireland. For these sins, he was doomed to die without ever setting foot in Ireland. His ship was wrecked at Skellig Island, off the coast of West Munster, and he died there.

As the first human being to die in Ireland, Donn became ruler of the human dead, and the Teach Duinn (The House of Donn), which some traditions place at Skellig Island, appears to have been originally another name for the Otherworld proper. The souls of the dead dwell there, spending their time in feasting and pleasures essentially identical to those I have described in Chapter 44.

Although the journey to the Otherworld is an important part of early Irish beliefs about death, it is not the only such belief. Many of the dead join the Daoine Síthe, going into the mounds, or become the Éarlaimh of the places where they have lived. This belief was very common among the Irish country people well into the 19th century, as illustrated by the testimony of Mr. John O'Conway, recorded sometime between 1900 and 1910:

> In olden times the Gentry (ie. the Daoine Síthe) were very numerous about forts and here on the Greenlands, but rarely seen. They appeared to be the same as any living men. When people died it was said the Gentry took them, for they would afterwards appear among the Gentry5.

According to the traditions of the Scottish Highlands, the evil dead do not go to any kind of hell, but become part of swarm of horrid aerial spirits known as the Sluagh, or "Host". These spirits fly through the air, perhaps repelled by the Earth, and, apparently, locked out of the Otherworld, as if trapped in transit between life and death. They owe their allegiance to the Fomoire, and so can be considered demonic spirits. Still, their state is not eternal, for if they are ever able to expiate their sins, they can return to a more desirable state. Alexander Carmichael describes them at length in Carmina Gadelica, in terms which bring to mind late 20th century folklore regarding everything from UFOs to cattle mutilations, to serial killers:

> The "hosts" are the spirits of mortals who have died…..According to one informant, the spirits fly about in great clouds, up and down the face of the world like starlings, and come back to the scenes of their Earthly transgressions……..nor can any win heaven until satisfaction is made for the sins of Earth……They fight battles in air as men do on Earth……..These spirits used to kill cats and dogs, sheep and cattle……..They commanded men to follow them, and men obeyed, having no alternative.
>
> It was these men of Earth who slew and maimed at he bidding of their spirit masters, who in turn ill-treated them in a most pitiless manner…..6

In addition to the afterlives already described, Irish Paganism also contains the belief in reincarnation, called **aithgen** in Irish, a word present in the Irish language from the earliest times[7]. Exactly who is reincarnated, and under what conditions, depends on the nature of each individual soul and its circumstances. Certainly, those people who have unfinished business in this world are likely to be quickly reborn. In addition, the majority of souls return with new life tasks. Only those who have accumulated sufficient bua, probably over several lives, can remain forever in the Otherworld, and become **Sinsir**, or ancestors.

There are examples of reincarnation in the Greco-Roman accounts, in the vernacular texts, and in the oral tradition. The Ulster king Mongan was said to be the reincarnation of Finn mac Cumhal, and was able to call on the spirit of the hero Caoilte to prove it[8]. In Tochmarc Étaíne (The Wooing of Étaín), we see another story of reincarnation, in which the Goddess Étaín is reborn as a human woman, and eventually recognized by her husband Midher[9]. Perhaps the most impressive example of such a story is that of Tuan mac Cairell, who was reborn as, among other things, a deer, a boar, a salmon, and a human chieftain, during which long succession of lives, he witnessed the entire history of the world[10].

In more modern times, the idea of reincarnation has still survived, although it is not often discussed. In about 1910, Steven Ruan, a well-known Galway piper, described the belief in reincarnation among some Irish country people:

> I have often heard it said that people born and dead come into this world again. I have hear the old people say that we lived on this Earth before; and I have often met old men and women who believed that they had lived before. The idea was passed from one old person to another, and was a common belief, though you do not hear much about it now[11].

**Interactions with the Dead:** Although the dead journey to the Otherworld, they do not entirely cease to interact with the living. As we have seen, the feast of Samhain includes a theme of hospitality for the dead, a welcoming of the dead, and sharing food with them. In addition, ancestors can be worshipped at other times, as needed or desired by individuals, and by the ancestors themselves. As we have seen ancestral spirits, who include most of the dead, are a recognized type of spiritual being, with their own powers, interests, and weaknesses. In general, of course, their personalities resemble those they had while alive, with those changes that could be naturally expected in a wholly novel environment12.

In addition, Ireland is the home of numerous ghost stories, and there can be little doubt that ghosts are part of the traditional Gaelic belief system. In fact, in Irish there are two words for "ghost", with quite different meanings.

The first term **taibhse** actually means appearance, and can be used, for example, to describe how someone looks. The sense here is that the appearance of a person or thing is somehow detached from the thing itself, and appears as a sort of free-floating apparition. In fact, this is a very useful concept, and can be used to describe, if not quite explain, that large class of ghost sightings in which the ghost simply carries out the same task over and over again, as it were mechanically, without any interactions with those who see it. Indeed, such apparitions have been reported to include inanimate objects and dead bodies, hardly likely to be forms of conscious spirits, but all too understandable if the taibhse can indeed endure after the real object has long vanished.

The second term for ghost is the more ordinary term **anam**, meaning soul or spirit. Here the concept is that of a spirit that has for some reason not gone on to the Otherworld or some other legitimate destination. There can be little doubt that such spirits have remained in this world for some reason peculiar to them, but, it would appear, such reasons are rarely valid or desirable in a value sense. Certainly, the fear with which ghosts are almost universally regarded, in Ireland as elsewhere, even though they are rarely, if ever physically dangerous, speaks to the essentially unnatural nature of the ghost as such. In any case, reports of such spirits, ghosts which do interact with the living, and do not mindlessly repeat the same scenes, are hardly confined to Ireland alone. In general, the Gaelic attitudes toward such spirits, beliefs about them, and methods of dealing with them are in no respect different from those of other peoples.

**Death Omens:** In modern society, death is almost always sudden and unannounced. In its anonymity, it is a terrifying example of the essential meaninglessness and helplessness of modern life. In our "free" society, we live at the mercy of unfathomable anonymous forces, that in time kill us, in the sterile confines of a hospital, with all the dignity of an animal in a slaughterhouse.

In the ancient and even recent Gaelic worlds, death was not like this. It was often preceded by signs, omens, and indications that the time had come[13]. Although frightening, these omens often gave time to prepare for death, and, more often, gave death a meaning which it lacks today. Death was not, and, in modern Irish Paganism, is not, as abrupt or disruptive an event to either the individual or the community. Rather, it is given a place, as something foretold, to some extent natural and planned, and part of the natural cycle of life. This cannot be the case for all deaths, of course. Some are genuinely tragic, events that should not have occurred, due to the influence of the Fomoire. But, the presence of death omens, and other similar beliefs, points the way to a reconciliation with death so far impossible in modern society.

Death omens are of many types, differing almost as much as the individuals who perceive them. They were very often reported, in one form or another, down to very recent times in the Highlands and the Irish countryside. Three rather typical examples include:

**Banshee (ie. Bean-sídhe, or Sídhe woman):** The Banshee is a death-spirit, usually attached to an individual family, whose keening predicts the death of a family member. Banshees can be of many difference appearances, ranging from great beauty to great ugliness. Banshees are **not** hostile spirits, and to not cause the deaths they foretell. They are of many different origins, though the majority are either human spirits or members of the Tuatha Dé Danann [14].

**Bodach Glas:** The Bodach Glas is said to act as a death omen. Unlike Banshees, they do not keen, nor are they connected to families, but appear to individuals more or less at random. They usually appear as people with dark gray skin, hair, and clothes, though this is not universal. Their origins are not known with any certainty[15].

**Bean Nighe:** The Bean Nighe, also called the Washing Woman or the Washer at the Ford, is a manifestation of the Mórrígan who appears in the ancient tales to warriors doomed to die. The doomed warrior will see her on the way to battle. He will notice an old woman washing clothes by a river side. When he looks more closely, he will see that they are bloodstained clothes. When he looks even more closely than that, he will see that the clothes are his, rent by the wounds of combat and death in war. Usually, the Washer disappears at this point, but in some tales, they may speak to the warrior, or even answer questions. In any case, the warrior now knows that he will not survive the battle, and that it is up to him to die as nobly as possible[16].

# *Glossary and Pronunciation Guide*

NOTE: for an even better dictionary of Irish Paganism, visit the Focloir Draiochta, at http://www.imbas.org/articles/focloir_draiochta.html

**Achainí (awch-un-ee):** invocation.
**Adhradh (AH-rah):** worship, from the Latin "adoratus"
**Aes Dàna (ayss DAW-na):** "men of art", the intellectual class of Ancient Ireland.
**Aíocht (EE-ocht):** generosity, hospitality, especially toward strangers.
**Airbhe (awrva):** hedge, magical barrier.
**Aithgen (awth-gen):** rebirth, reincarnation.
**Altramas (AWL-tramus):** Fosterage.
**Anam (awn-um):** soul.
**Balor (bal-or):** a name for the King of the Fomoire. See also Crom Cruaich and Crom Dubh.
**Bandia (BAWN-juh):** "Woman God", Goddess.
**Bealach d'aimhleasa (BYAL-ach DOW-lessa):** "the road to ruin", a bad path in life.
**Bealtaine (bel-tuh-nuh):** May Day, the beginning of summer, the second holiest day of the year, usually on or about May 1.
**Beannacht:** blessing.
**Beirmhíol (bear-veel):** A Nascmhíol connected to a person through his or her true name. See Nascmhíol below.
**Bile (beel-yuh):** big tree, also used for the World Tree.
**Bliain (blee-un):** year, including the yearly calendar of festivals (and all the other usual connoations of the word "year").

**Brat (brawt):** mantle, cloak, blanket, really an article of clothing that is all of these at once, and is one of the most important in early Irish culture.
**Breitheamh (BRE-hev), plural Breithiúna (BRE-hoona):** Judge, jurist.
**Bres (bres):** a Fomor who became ruler of the Tuatha Dé Danann and subjected them to great oppression. He was deposed after being satirized for his lack of generosity.
**Brugh na Boine (broo na boin):** Newgrange Tumulus, north of Dublin on the Boyne River, known in legend as the home of the Dagda and Angus mac Óg, among others.
**Bua (boo-uh):** virtue, victory, strength, and spiritual power.
**Cailleach (CAWL-yach):** literally "veiled one", but meaning an old woman or a crone. Can also be used for a type of local Land Goddess found in many locations.
**Calmacht (CAL-macht):** hardiness, endurance.
**Carmina Gadelica:** "Songs of the Gael", a collection of charms, incantations, prayers, and other forms of oral poetry collected by Alexander Carmichael in the Scottish Highlands in the mid 19th century.
**Ceart (cyart):** right, just, morally just, correct, proper, good, true, real. From Latin Certus.
**Céile (CAYL-uh), plural Céilte (CAYL-tuh):** client, companion, spouse.
**Céilsine (CAYL-shin-uh):** cliency.
**Ceolteor (CEL-tor), plural Ceolteori (CEL-tori):** musician.
**Cineàl (KIN-all), plural Cineàlacha (KIN-all-acha):** kindred, kin-group, family, dynasty, race, kind, type, territory.
**Claenmhíol (clawn-veel):** The Nascmhíol of a tribe or family. See Nascmhíol below.
**Claíomh (cleave):** sword.
**Cleathansai (cla-han-see):** paraphernalia, stuff, magical tools.
**Cneastacht (c'NEST-acht):** sincerity, inner integrity, wholeness.
**Coibche (KIV-shuh):** bride price, see also Tionscra below.
**Cóir (core):** justice, just, in accord with Fírinne.
**Coire (corra):** cauldron.
**Conchobar (CON-co-vor):** King of Ulster during the Tain Bo Cualigne, patron of Cuchulainn, and a figure of many legends. He is at once heroic and villainous.
**Corr Bolg (corr voll-eg):** "Crane Bag", a bag used by Manannan to store magical treasures that was larger on the inside than on the outside, by extension, any bag used to store sacred items.
**Corrguinacht (COR-gyun-acht):** "Crane Magic", the art of cursing encircling an enemy on one foot, with one eye closed, and one arm

extended while chanting mallacht.

**Craobh Cheoil (croyv chyoil):** musical branch, a branch strung with bells, one of the chief symbols of the poets office and a symbol of the Otherworld, used to produce trance as well as chair meetings.

**Crógacht (CRO-gacht):** ferocity, blood-thirst

**Crom Cruaich (crom croo-ach):** "Bent One of the Mound", a name for the King of the Fomoire. See also Balor and Crom Dubh.

**Crom Dubh (crom doo OR crom duv):** "Bent Black One", a name for the King of the Fomoire. See also Balor and Crom Cruaich.

**Cuchulainn (COO-hoo-lin):** a great warrior from Ancient Ulster, son of Lugh, and hero of the Tain Bo Cualigne.

**Dàn (dawn):** fate, destiny, art, talent.

**Daoine Síthe (Deeny Shee):** Really just a term for the Síthe (see below), but I am also using it as a generic term for nature spirits.

**De ocus an-de (jay okus un-jay):** Old Irish form of Déithe agus an-Déithe.

**Dealbh (jel-ev):** image, "idol", statue.

**Deireadh (jerry):** end.

**Déithe Adhartha (JAY-huh a-yar-'ha):** "Gods of Worship", a term for the Pagan Irish Gods that I am using for the greater deities.

**Déithe agus an-Déithe (JAY-huh ag-us an-JAY-huh):** "Gods and not-Gods", a traditional designation for the Tuatha Dé Danann meaning essentially "Gods and Spirits".

**Déithe Danann (JAY-huh DAWN-unn):** My term for craft deities, taken from *Tri De Danann* (see below).

**Dia (juh), plural Déithe (JAY-huh):** God, deity, "shining one".

**Diach (DEE-ach):** misfortune, bad karma.

**Dícheadal (DEECH-e-jal):** incantation, galdor.

**Dilseacht (DIL-shecht):** loyalty, troth.

**Dlúth (dlukh):** warp, weave, the inner nature of a person or thing.

**Domhain (da-wan):** the Abyss, the deep, the realm of the Fomoire.

**Draoi (dree), plural Draoithe (dree-yuh):** sorcerer, magician, holy person, druid, priest/ess.

**Draíocht (DREE-awcht):** magic, druidry, sorcery, the magical traditions of the Ancient Irish.

**Dualgas (DOOL-'gahs):** duty, right.

**Éarlamh (AIR-lav), plural Éarlaimh (AIR-lawv):** patron deity of a place, district, tribe, or major geographical feature.

**Echtrai (ech-tree):** "Adventures", class of Irish traditional stories involving accidental visits to the Otherworld.

**Éric (AY-ric):** blood price, the price paid for a particular injury or offense.

**Fàidh (faw), plural Fàithe (FOY-yuh):** prophet, seer, sage.
**Fénechas (FAYN-uh-chus):** The Ancient Irish Laws, also called the Brehon Laws. The term means "Law of the Land Tillers".
**File (FEE-luh), plural Filí (FEE-lee):** poet, sorcerer, prophet.
**Filidecht:** older spelling of Filíocht.
**Filíocht (FEE-lee-ocht):** poetry, poetic art, the magic of the poet, including prophecy, spells, satires, and so on. The work of Erynn Laurie provides a good guide to this.
**Fine (FIN-nuh), plural Finnte (FIN-tuh):** family, family lineage.
**Finn mac Cumhail (finn mac cool):** a great warrior, magician, sage, and outlaw, among other things. Possibly the greatest hero in Irish mythology.
**Fios (feess):** knowledge, wisdom, in ancient times especially occult wisdom.
**Fir Bolg (feer bawl-'g):** a race of spirit beings who inhabited the world before the Tuatha Dé Danann, and who were defeated by the Tuatha Dé Danann when they entered this world. Various Irish families are in fact descended from them, as are many spirits.
**Fírinne (feer-in-na):** Cosmic Truth, cosmic order, the fitness of things.
**Flaithiúlacht (FLAW-hyul-acht):** generosity, lavishness.
**Fomor (fo-mor), plural Fomoire (fo-moir-uh):** the race of deformed giants or demons opposed to the Tuatha Dé Danann, representing chaos, darkness, and calamity.
**Geis (gaysh), plural Gessa (gessa):** a ritual prohibition or injunction, usually forbidding a particular activity, often related to "totem" animals, or to one's dlúth.
**Gó (go):** falsehood, lies, deceit, the opposite of Firinne.
**Idircheo (ider-chyo):** "Between Mists", the barriers between this world and the Otherworld.
**Iloireadas (il-or-uh-jus):** lack of correspondence between this world and the Otherworld in terms of time and space.
**Imbolc (immulk):** the Festival of Brigid, on or about February 2.
**Imramma (im-rawm-a):** "Voyages", class of Irish traditional story involving voyages to the Otherworld, usually by crossing the ocean.
**Íobairt (EE-vawrt):** sacrifice, offering.
**Ionraicas (IN-'rawc-us):** integrity, uprightness.
**Íonú (ee-noo):** purification.
**Lànamnas (LAW-num-nus):** Old Irish term for marriage.
**Lia (lee-uh):** understone.
**Log n'oineach (LOY NYEN-ech):** honor price, the value set on insult to a person based on his/her rank and honor.

**Lughnasadh (loo-na-sah) also spelled Lughnasa:** the Festival of Lugh and the beginning of the harvest, usually on or about August 1.
**Macànta (MUCK-awnta):** gentleness, kindness, guilelessness.
**Mag Tuired (moy toora):** a plain in Ireland that was the site of two battles, the first between the Tuatha Dé Danann and the Fir Bolg, the second between the Tuatha Dé Danann and the Fomoire.
**Mallacht (mal-acht):** cursing, magic intended to cause harm.
**Midher (meer):** one of the Tuatha Dé Danann, known for losing and then regaining his wife, Etain, and for various other adventures. His animals are three cranes.
**Misneach (MISH-nech):** courage, keeping a level head.
**Muince (moo-ink-uh):** neckring, torc.
**Naofa (nayva):** holy, pious, sacred, sanctified, dignified, eminent, of high rank or status.
**Nascmhíol (NASK-veel):** "totem" animal, an animal linked in some way to the dlúth or the soul of a person.
**Neimheadh (NAY-va):** 1. a sacred place, sanctuary, or temple space. 2. king of an ancient spirit race, ancestors of the Tuatha Dé Danann and also humanity, husband to Macha.
**Oineach (EN-ech):** literally "face", by extension honor, esteem, reputation, status.
**Samhain (sow-un):** Halloween, All Souls Day, the Celtic New Year, the holiest day of the year, usually on or about November 1.
**Scian (skee-un):** knife.
**Seanchaí (SHYAN-'chee), plural Seanchaithe (SHYAN-'chee-yuh):** keeper of tradition, reciter of ancient lore, traditional storyteller, genealogist, historian.
**Seanchas (SHEN-'chus):** tradition, traditional lore, traditional law, genealogical lore, conversation, discourse.
**Sí (Shee):** Fairy mound, by extension a fairy being or any kind of Irish spirit being, including the Tuatha Dé Danann, among other races of spirit beings.
**Sinsear (SIN-ser), plural Sinsir (SIN-seer):** Ancestor.
**Slàn (slawn):** healthy, safe, sound, whole, complete, intact, perfect, holy, secure.
**Slànú (slaw-noo):** saving, salvation, rescue.
**Slat (slawt):** wand.
**Sleà (slaw):** spear.
**Slí (slee):** way, path, profession.
**Smúrchoigilt (SMOOR-cho-gilt):** "smooring", the act of banking a fire and smoothing over the ashes.

**Taibhse (toyv-shuh):** apparition, appearance.
**Tairise (TAWR-isha):** reliability, steadfastness, dependability.
**Teallach (TYEL-ach):** hearth, I also use it to mean "coven".
**Teorainn (tor-oin):** boundary, border.
**Tine Chnàimhe (tin-uh chnaiv):** "bone fire", sacred fire.
**Tionscra (TINN-uh-scra):** groom price, see also coibche above.
**Tir na'n Óg (teer nan oag):** "Land of the Young", one of several names for the paradiscal Otherworld.
**Tir no Fhuin (teer no hoo-in):** The Land Under Wave, sometimes a synonym for the Otherworld, other times inhabited by Merrows and other undersea beings.
**Tuan mac Cairell (too-un mac car-el):** the real founder of Irish Paganism, a chieftain who entered the world at its very beginning and was then reincarnated through various forms throughout its history, remembering all that happened to him, most especially the tales of the history of the world before human kind, including those of the Tuatha Dé Danann.
**Tobar (taw-bur):** well, spring.
**Tri De Danann (Tree jay DAWN-unn):** "Three Gods of Art", a trio of craft deities, with various members in different sources.
**Tri Mórrígna (tree MAWR-eeg-na):** "Three Great Queens", or "Three Morrigans", a trio of war, fertility, fate, sovereignty Goddesses. Confusingly, different accounts give it different members.
**Troclaigh (TROK-lee):** fasting in order to compel a powerful person to admit wrongdoing.
**Tuath (too-ath), plural Tuatha (too-uh-huh):** a tribe, a folk, a people, usually at least semi-autonomous, with a common sense of kinship and spiritual identity.
**Tuatha Dé Danann (Too-uh-huh jay dawn-un):** The Gods and Spirits of Ancient Ireland, the Irish Gods.
**Uisce Naofa (ooshka nay-va):** holy water.
**Urnaí (orr-nee), plural Urnaithe (oor-nee-yuh):** prayer.

# *Appendix A*
# Íobairt ina Gaelige

H. Íonú
I. Beannacht na'n Neimheadh
   a. Déanamh na'n Thine Chnáimhe:
         Is tusa an croi na'n saol,
      thine chnáimhe chead ó thus na t-am.
        Is tusa an solas na Greine
      ce a dhealaigh an la as an oiche.
      Is tusa an thine na gach Teallach,
       's gach tine ag teacht ó tusa.
        Is tusa an solas na'n anam
         ce ata i gach daoine.
    Dean me tusa, a-thine, ina chaoi na Brigid
       anseo air an Teallach naofa.

   b. Déanamh na'n Uisce Naofa
       Is tusa an mhaithar na na déithe,
         tobar na gach beatha.
       Is tusa an tobar na gach feasa,
         Bandia na'n Iomas.
       Is tusa an Bhandia na ghra,
   An bhean-tiarna a chur beatha isteach i'n saol.
       Is tusa bean-tiarna na'n thir,
        Bandia na'n flaitheas.
     Gan tusa, nil muide ach dada;
       le tusa, ta muide lan.

   c. Déanamh na'n Airbhe

III. **Íobairt fein**
      d. Achainí
      e. Dícheadal
V.   **Deireadh na'n Íobairt**
    A.   **Slánú na'n Uisce Beatha:**

> Is tusa an mhaithar na na déithe,
> Tobar na gach beatha.
> Is tusa tobar na gach feasa,
> Bandia na'n Iomas.
> Is tusa an Bhandia na ghra,
> An Bhean-tiarna a-chur beatha isteach i'n saol.
> Is tusa bean-tiarna na'n Thir,
> Bandia na'n Flaitheas.
> Slanaigh me tusa isTéach me fein
> Gur a bheith tusa linn riamh.

    B.   **Smúrchoigilt na'n Thine Chnáimhe:**

> Is tusa an croi na'n saol,
> Thine chnáimhe chead, ó thus na t-am.
> Is tusa an solas na Greine
> Ce a dhealaigh an la as an oiche.
> Is tusa an thine na gach Teallach,
> 's gach tine ag teacht ó tusa.
> Is tusa an solas na'n anam,
> Ce ata I gach daoine.
> Slánaigh me thusa, a-thine, ina chaoi na Brigid,
> Anseo i'n teallach naofa.

    C.   **An Deireadh:**

> Ta an íobairt deanta
> Daoine 's déithe
> Dulaige muide as an Neimheadh
> Neartach 's lan
> Le gra in ár gcroithe.

# Appendix B
# Invocations in English and Irish

**Invocation To the Mórrígan**

A Mhórríghan Mhor
A Bhantiarna na'n Dán
A Bhantiarna na'n Fhaistine
A Bhantiarna na'n Oiche
Tar anocht!

A Mhórríghan Bhuach
A Rioghan na'n Cath
A Rioghan na'n Bhuile
A Rioghan na'n Fiach
Tar anocht!

Tar do'n Neimheadh againn
's muide ag chur oineach duit.

Great Mórrígan
Lady of Fate
Lady of Prophecy
Lady of the Night
Come tonight!

Victorious Mórrígan

> Queen of Battles
> Queen of Frenzies
> Queen of Ravens
> Come tonight!
>
> Come to our neimheadh
> Where we are giving you honor!

**Invocation To Dánu:**

> A Dhánnan, a Mhathair
> A Mhathair na na Déithe
> A Mhathair na'n Tobar
> A Mhathair na'n Cothú
> Tar anocht!
>
> A Dhánann, a Mhathair
> A Thabharthóir na'n Fios
> A Thabharthóir na'n Blath
> A Tabharthóir na Bheatha
> Tar anocht!
>
> Tar do'n Neimheadh againn
> 's muide ag chur oineach duit!
>
> Mother Dánu
> Mother of the Gods
> Mother of the Well
> Mother of Nurturing
> Come tonight!
>
> Mother Dánu
> Giver of Wisdom
> Giver of Prosperity
> Giver of Life
> Come Tonight!
>
> Come to our neimheadh
> Where we are giving you honor!

**Invocation To Macha:**

A-Mhacha a-Rioghan
A Mhacha Mong Rua
A Mhacha ni Sanrith
A Mhacha Bean Cheile na Neimheadh
Tar anocht!

A Mhacha, a Rioghan
A Bheantiarna na'n Flaitheas
A Bheantiarna na'n Talamh
A Bheantirna na'n t-Each
Tar anocht!

Tar do'n Neimheadh againn
's muide ag chur oineach duit!

Queen Macha
Macha of the Red Tresses
Macha ni Sanrith
Macha Wife of Nemed
Come tonight!

Queen Macha
Lady of Sovereignty
Lady of the Earth
Lady of the Horse
Come tonight!

Come to our Neimheadh
Where we will give you honor!

**Invocation To Lugh**

A Lugh, a Ardtiarna
A Lugh Lamhfhada
A Lugh Samildánach
A Lugh Marfóir na Balor
Tar anocht!

A Lugh, a Ardtiarna
A Dhia na'n Thintreach
A Dhia a chur an Fómhar
A Dhia na'n tSlea

Tar anocht!

Tar do'n Neimheadh againn
's muide ag chur oineach duit!

Lord Lugh
Lugh Lamhfhada
Lugh Samildánach
Lugh, Slayer of Balor
Come tonight!

Lord Lugh
God of Lightning
God who gives the Harvest
God with the Spear
Come tonight!

Come to our Neimheadh
Where we are giving you honor!

**Invocation To Nuada**

A Nuada, a Aire
A Nuada Argetlamh
A Nuada Necht
A Nuada na'n Ceo
Tar anocht!

A Nuada, A Aire
A Dhia na'n Theorainn
A Dhia na'n Laoch
A Dhia na'n Claíomh
Tar anocht!

Tar do'n Neimheadh againn
's muide ag chur oineach duit!

Lord Nuada
Nuada Silver Hand
Nuada Necht
Nuada of the Mists
Come tonight!

Lord Nuada
God of Boundaries
God of Warriors
God of the Sword
Come tonight!

Come to our Neimheadh
Where we are giving you honor!

**Invocation To the Dagda**

A Dhagda Mor
A Eochaidh Ollathair
A Ruaidh Rofhessa
A Áedh
Tar anocht!

A Dhagda na'n Neamh
A Dhia le'n Coire
A Dhia le'n Chláirseach
A Dhia le'n Ord
Tar anocht!

Tar do'n Neimheadh againn
's muide ag chur oineach duit!

Great Dagda
Eochaidh Allfather
Red One of Great Knowledge
Flame
Come tonight!

Dagda of the Heavens
God of the Cauldron
God of the Harp
God of the Hammer
Come tonight!

Come to our Neimheadh
Where we are giving you honor!

**Invocation To Áine**

A Áine Lonrach

A Bhé na'n Ghrian
A Bhé ina Bláth
A Bhé na'n Maidhneachan
Tar anocht!

A Áine Lonrach
A Bhandia na'n Ghraidh
A Bhandia na Méan Samhradh
A Bhandia na'n Solas
Tar anocht!

Tar do'n neimheadh againn
's muide ag chur oineach duit!

Shining Áine
Maiden of the Sun
Maiden in Blossom
Maiden of Dawn
Come tonight!

Shining Áine
Goddess of Love
Goddess of Midsummer
Goddess of Light
Come tonight!

Come to our neimheadh
Where we will give you blessing!

**Invocation To Brigid**

A Bhrigid A Bhandia
A Bhandia na'n Teallach
A Bhandia na'n Thine
A Bhandia is brea
Tar anocht!

A Bhrigid naofa
A Bheantiarna na'n Fhíliocht
A Bheantiarna na'n Dán na'n Gabha
A Bheantiarna na'n Dán na'n Lia
Tar anocht!

Tar do'n Neimheadh againn
's muide ag chur oineach duit!

Holy Brigid
Goddess of the Hearth
Goddess of Fire
Goddess most excellent
Come tonight!

Goddess Brigid
Lady of Poetry
Lady of Smithcraft
Lady of Healing
Come tonight!

Come to our Neimheadh
Where we are giving you honor!

**Invocation To Manannán:**

A Mhanannain Gaoiseach
A Mhac an Toinn
A Dhia na Reannáin
A Dhia na Loingis
Tar anocht!

A Mhanannain Gaoiseach
A Chomhdeoir na Ceannaithe
A Chomhdeoir na Taistealaithe
A Oscloir na'n Shli
Tar anocht!

Tar do'n Neimheadh againn
's muide ag chur oineach duit!

Wise Manannán
Son of the Wave
God of Headlands
God of Ships
Come tonight!

Wise Manannán
Protector of Merchants
Protector of Travelers

Opener of the Way
Come tonight!

Come to our Neimheadh
Where we are giving you blessing!

**Invocation To Angus Og**

A Angus na'n Brugh
A Mhac Og
A Mhac na'n Dhraíocht
A Mhac na'n Ghra
Tar anocht!

A Angus na'n Mealladh
A Dhia le'n Brat na'n Dhofheictheacht
A Dhia le'n Triur Éin
A Dhia na'n Samhradh
Tar anocht!

Tar do'n Neimheadh againn
's muide ag chur oineach duit!

Angus of the Brudh
Son of the Young
Son of Magic
Son of Love
Come tonight!

Angus of the Glamours
God with the Cloak of Invisibility
God with the Three Birds
God of Summer
Come tonight!

Come to our Neimheadh
Where we are giving you honor!

**Invocation To Boann**

A Bhoann Naofa
A Bheantiarna na'n Gheallach
A Bheantiarna na'n Thaoide
A Bheantiarna na t-Am

Tar anocht!

A Bhoann na'n tSpeir
A Bhandia na'n Bhó
A Bhandia na'n Bhoinne
A Bhandia na'n Aibhainn na Neamh
Tar anocht!

Tar do'n Neimheadh againn
's muide ag chur oineach duit!

Holy Boann
Lady of the Moon
Lady of the Tide
Lady of Time
Come tonight!

Boann of the Sky
Goddess of the Cow
Goddess of the Boyne
Goddess of the River of Heaven
Come tonight!

Come to our Neimheadh
Where we are giving you blessing!

# *Appendix C*
# Organizations, Websites, and Leaders

### Celtic Reconstructionist:

Paganacht – A general portal to the Celtic Reconstructionist community on the web, the Paganacht website includes the CR FAQ, which can also be found on the Witches' Voice, as well as a number of articles by various CR elders, and a link to the Páganachd journal on LiveJournal. http://www.paganacht.com

Livejournal has a Celtic Reconstructionist community called cr_r, which can be accessed at http://www.livejournal.com/userinfo.bml?user=cr_r

Members participate in mostly civil, often scholarly, and sometimes practical discussions of Celtic Reconstructionist ideas and practice.

**The Imbas Website:** Imbas no longer exists as an organization, but their excellent introductory website still does. Definitely worth a look. http://www.imbas.org

**The Imbas-public list:** The public discussion list also survived the demise of Imbas as an organization. It remains extremely active, an important center of CR thought. http://groups.yahoo.com/group/imbas-public/

**The Deiuokara Website:** Another CR tradition, different from the Paganacht of Kym, Kathryn and friends, or the Senistrognatha of Imbas, Deiuokara was organized by Tearlach Roibeard Luder, who was for years the moderator of the Celtic Nation list, where some important discussions and arguments have taken place. http://www.deiuokara.com

## Neo-Druidic:

**Druid Order of the Whiteoak:** This is Ellen Evert Hopman's Reconstructionist Druid organization **Ord na Darach Gile**, which represents a tradition midway between CR and Neodruidism. I can vouch for the fact that Ellen is dedicated, scholarly, and ethical whenever I have dealt with her, and that her organization, last I had anything to do with it, was of high quality. http://www.whiteoakdruids.org

**Ar nDraiocht Fein:** An Indo-European Druid organization founded by Isaac Bonewits in 1985, ADF has had a profound influence of Celtic Paganism since its inception. http://www.adf.org

**The Henge of Keltria:** This group split amicably from ADF in order to pursue a more Celtic path, back in the mid-80s. For a time, in the early '90s, it was the center of some very interesting scholarship and discussion. http://www.keltria.org

# *Appendix D*
# Non-Pagan Cultural and Language Websites

**Daltaí na Gailige:** A website and non-profit organization dedicated to teaching the Irish language and helping language students. Lots of good resources, including language classes in various parts of the United States and Canada. http://www.daltai.com

**Gael-Linn:** An old, well established organization in Ireland, aimed at promoting Irish Gaelic language and culture. http://www.gael-linn.ie/

**Sabhal Mór Ostaig:** The Scottish Gaelic college on the Isle of Skye. Scots Gaelic resources. http://www.smo.uhi.ac.uk

**Clí Gáidhlig:** Scots Gaelic learning site and clearinghouse, promoting access to the Scots Gaelic language. http://www.cli.org.uk/

**Celtic Studies Resources:** Just what the name says, a collection of resources devoted to Celtic studies. http://www.digitalmedievalist.com

**Celtic League American Branch:** The active New York-based American branch of the famous Celtic League, a pan-Celtic cultural and nationalist organization. http://www.celticleague.org

**CELT – Corpus of Electronic Texts:** A collection of Irish texts, from the middle ages to modern times. An excellent resource. http://www.ucc.ie/celt

# Notes

## Notes to Chapter 2

1. Foclóir Gaelige-Béarla / Niall Ó Dónaill – [Baile Átha Cliath]: An Gúm, c1977, 1992 p. 398
2. Idem
3. Ibid, p. 84
4. University of Wales Center for Advanced Welsh and Celtic Studies – Celtic lexicon – http://www.aber.ac.uk/~awcwww/PCI_MoE.pdf See also Labarion-English Dictionary – http://p3.grp.yahoofs.com/v1/cPBtQONéitum
5. The American Heritage Dictionary of Indo-European Roots – Second Edition/ Revised and Edited by Calvert Watkins – Boston: Houghtoin-Mifflin, c2000, p. 22
6. Foclóir Gaelige-Béarla, p. 8
7. "Dánu and Bile: the primordial parents?" / Alexei Kondratiev: An Tríbhís Mhór, vol. 1, no. 2 – Montague, NJ: Imbas, Bealtaine, 1998, p57-61
8. A dictionary of Celtic mythology / James MacKillop – [Oxford]: Oxford University Press, c1998 p. 16
9. Idem
10. Irish Texts Society, vol. XLI Lebor Gabála Érenn: part 4 / edited and translated by RAS Macallister – Dublin, 1941 p. 182-183, 188-189
11. Ibid, p. 188-189
12. Loc Cit

13. An encyclopedia of fairies: hobogoblins, brownies, bogies, and other supernatural creatures / Katherine Briggs – New York: Pantheon, c1976 p. 58-60
14. Idem
15. MacKillop, p. 16
16. Ibid, p. 335-337
17. Idem, also ibid, p. 334-335
18. A guide to Irish mythology / Daragh Smyth – [Dublin]: Irish Academic, c1988, 1996 p. 125-127
19. Loc Cit
20. War Goddess: the Morrígan and her Germano-Celtic counterparts / by Angelique Gulermovich Epstein – Los Angeles: University of California Los Angeles, 1998, p57-61
21. Cath Maige Tuired: the $2^{nd}$ Battle of Mag Tuired/ edited by Elizabeth A. Gray – Dublin: Irish Texts Society, 1982 p. 44-45
22. Idem
23. Smyth, p. 125-127
24. Ibid, p. 70-73
25. Epstein, p. 101-102
26. MacKillop, p. 334-337
27. Smyth, p. 125-127
28. MacKillop, p. 335-337
29. LocCit
30. Idem
31. Idem
32. Idem
33. Idem
34. Epstein, p. 54-57
35. MacKillop, p. 335-337
36. Ibid, p. 334-335. "Great Sacred" is my own conjectural translation from the Gaulish.
37. Epstein, p. 57-61
38. Briggs, Encyclopedia, p.. 19-20
39. Irish Texts Society, v. XLIX Táin Bo Cúaligne/ edited by Cecile O'Rahilly – Dublin: Irish Texts Society, 1967 p. 127
40. MacKillop, p. 318-319
41. Smyth, p. 105-107
42. MacKillop, p. 318
43. Irish Texts Society, v. XXXIX Lebor Gabála Érenn:, part III/ edited and translated by RAS Macallister – Dublin: Irish Texts Society, 1941 p.132-133

44. Poems from the Dindsenchas: text, translation, and vocabulary – Royal Irish Academy Todd Lecture Series, Vol. II/ by Edward Gwynne – Dublin: Academy House, 1900, p. 14-20
45. Smyth, p. 35, 105-107
46. MacKillop, p. 190, 318
47. Smyth, p. 105-107
48. Idem
49. Idem
50. Basic Celtic Deity Types/ Alexei Kondratiev - copyright and copy, 1997 Alexei Kondratiev. Internet document, no longer extant to my knowledge.
51. Lugus/ Chrisopher Gwinn, copyright 2000, Christopher Gwinn. Internet document, no longer extant to my knowledge.
52. Smyth, p. 102-104
53. MacKillop, p. 306
54. Smyth, p. 102-104
55. Idem
56. Idem
57. Cath Maige Tuired, p. 38-39
58. Ibid, p. 38-43
59. Idem
60. Ibid, p. 60-63
61. Smyth, p. 102-104
62. Kondratiev, Basic Celtic Deity Types
63. Idem
64. Idem
65. Idem
66. Smyth, p. 102-104
67. Idem
68. Lugus: the many skilled lord/ Alexei Kondratiev – internet document, no longer extant to my knowledge
69. Loc Cit
70. Ibid, p. 130-132
71. MacKillop, p. 348-349
72. Cath Maige Tuired, p. 38-43
73. Kondratiev, Basic Celtic Deity Types
74. The Apple Branch: a path to Celtic ritual/ Alexei Kondratiev – [Cork, Ireland: Collins Press], c1998, p. 79-88
75. Loc Cit
76. Smyth, p. 130-132
77. MacKillop, p. 125-126

78. Smyth, p. 48-49
79. Cath Maige Tuired, p. 44-51
80. Smyth, p. 48-49
81. Idem
82. Cath Maige Tuired, p. 70-71
83. Op Cit, p. 125-127
84. Ibid, p. 48-49
85. Idem
86. MacKillop, p. 58-59
87. Carmina Gadelica: hymns and incantations,: with illustrative notes on wards, rites, and customs dying and obsolete/ orally collected in the Highlands and Islands of Scotland by Alexander Carmichael – [Hudson, NY]: Lindisfarne, c1992 (republication) p. 81, 580-586
88. Loc Cit, also MacKillop, p. 58
89. MacKillop, p. 58-59
90. Idem
91. Smyth, p. 28-29
92. Carmichael, 580-586
93. Op Cit, p. 28-30
94. The Year in Ireland/ by Kevin Dánaher – [Dublin]: Mercier, c1972, p. 13-31
95. Op Cit, p. 28-29
96. Idem
97. Ibid, p. 18-19
98. Idem
99. MacKillop, p. 10
100. Idem
101. Dánaher, 134-135
102. Smyth, p. 18-19
103. Celtic Gods, Celtic Goddesses/ RJ Stewart, illustrated by Miranda Grey and Courtney Davis – [London]: Blandford, c1990 p. 121-122
104. MacKillop, p. 10
105. Smyth, p. 111-113
106. Ibid, p. 87-88
107. Celtic heritage: ancient tradition in Ireland and Wales/ Alwyn and Brinley Rees – [New York]: Thames and Hudson, c1961, p. 315-316
108. Op Cit, p. 111-113
109. This practice was to my knowledge originated in the literature and practice of Ar nDraiocht Fein, a NeoDruid group that still exists. It

has been carried on by Celtic Pagan and Druid groups in the years since.
110. Loc Cit
111. Loc Cit
112. Loc Cit
113. MacKillop, p. 110
114. Loc Cit
115. Idem
116. Maponus/ by Christopher Gwinn – copyright, 2001
117. MacKillop, p. 17-18
118. Idem
119. Smyth, p. 15-16
120. Idem
121. Idem
122. Idem
123. Ibid, p. 22-23
124. Idem
125. MacKillop, p. 45
126. Loc Cit
127. MacKillop, p. 351-352
128. Idem
129. Smyth p. 135-136
130. Loc Cit
131. Idem
132. Idem
133. Idem
134. Idem
135. Foclóir Gaelige-Béarla, p. 598
136. Op Cit., p. 80-82
137. Idem
138. MacKillop, p. 255-256
139. Dictionary of Celtic myth and legend/ Miranda J. Green – [New York]: Thames and Hudson, c1992 p. 193-195
140. Smyth, p. 81
141. MacKillop, p. 138
142. Lincoln, p. 181-184
143. private email from Alexei Kondratiev, no longer extant
144. Early Medieval Ireland: 400 – 1200 – Longman History of Ireland Series/ Daibhi Ó Croinin – Boston: Addison Wesley, 1995, p. 38
145. MacKillop, p. 4
146. Green, Dictionary, p. 62

147. Smyth, p. 36
148. Dindsenchus, p. 1-28
149. Loc Cit
150. Smyth, p. 36
151. Dindsenchus, p. 348-356
152. Ibid, p. 460-469
153. Ibid, p. 356-376
154. Smyth, p. 74-75
155. Green, Dictionary, p. 159-160
156. MacKillop, p. 387
157. Gods and heroes of the Celts/ Marie-Louise Sjoestedt, translated by Myles Dillon – Berekley, CA: Turtle Island Foundation, 1982 p.44
158. MacKillop, p. 406-407
159. Smyth, p. 16-18
160. Op Cit, p. 10-11
161. Op Cit, p. 31-32
162. Ibid, p. 32
163. Ibid, p. 92-94
164. Ibid, p. 102-104
165. MacKillop, p. 322-323
166. Op Cit, p. 119-120
167. Ibid, p. 127-128
168. Ibid, p. 129-130
169. Ibid, p. 130-132
170. Ibid, p. 155
171. see pages 29-30
172. The sacred cauldron: secrets of the Druids/ Tadhg MacCrossan – St. Paul, MN: Llewellyn, 1991, p. 170-171
173. Briggs, Encyclopedia, 335-336
174. MacKillop, p. 147-148
175. Death, war, and sacrifice: studies in ideology and practice/ Bruce Lincoln; forward by Wendy Doniger – Chicago: University of Chicago Press, c1991 p. 32-48
176. Idem
177. MacKillop, p. 147-148
178. Loc Cit
179. Robert Kirk: walker between worlds: a new edition of the secret commonwealth of elves, fauns, and fairies/ RJ Stewart – Shaftesbury, Dorset: Element Books, c1990 p. 21-23, 28-29
180. Briggs, Encyclopedia, p. 96-97, 135
181. MacKillop, p. 234-235

182. Op Cit, p. 393-394
183. Ibid, p. 69-72
184. Ibid, p. 127
185. Stewart, Robert Kirk, p. 26
186. Op Cit, p. 25-27
187. Ibid, p. 335-336
188. Earth light: the ancient path to transformation: rediscovering the wisdom of ancient Celtic and Faerie lore/ RJ Stewart – Rockport, MA: Element, c1992 p.29-30; also Briggs, Encyclopedia, p. 145-147, 151-153, 378-380
189. Briggs, Encyclopedia, p. 25
190. The vanishing people: Fairy lore and legends/ Katherine Briggs, illustrations by Mary French – New York, Pantheon c1978 p. 53-56
191. Briggs, Encyclopedia, p. 44-45 for one example, also Briggs, Vanishing people, p. 66-80
192. Briggs, Encyclopedia, p. 290-294
193. Ibid, , p. 177
194. Ibid, p. 254-256
195. Ibid, p. 349-350, 353-355, 340-341
196. Ibid, p. 134-135
197. Ibid, p. 104-106, 185
198. Ibid, p. 383-385
199. This version is from Briggs, Vanishing people, p. 154-156
200. Op Cit, p. 159-161
201. Ibid, p. 287-290, 443-445

## Notes to Chapter 3

1. Foclóir Draíochta – Dictionary of Druidism/ by Sean Ó Tuathail – copyright 1993 John Kellnhauser/CainTéanna na Luise, p. 9.
2. This is my own extension of Ó Tuathail's concept.
3. Loc Cit
4. Ibid, p. 6
5. Ibid, p. 16
6. Celtic Values/ Alexei Kondratiev – internet document. This is from an earlier version (ca. 1995) than the one currently widely available on the internet. Kondratiev's material in this case was also modified by me based on Ó Dónaill, Foclóir Gaelige-Béarla, various pages and entries.
7. Idem

## Notes

8. Idem
9. Idem
10. Idem
11. Idem
12. Idem
13. Idem
14. Idem
15. Idem
16. Idem
17. Idem
18. Idem
19. Idem
20. Ó Tuathail, p. 3
21. Ibid, p. 1
22. Ibid, p. 6
23. Ibid, p. 10
24. Ibid, p. 4
25. Idem
26. Idem
27. Green, Dictionary, p. 41
28. Kondratiev, Apple Branch, p. 81-82, 194-198, 260
29. Op Cit, p. 51-52
30. Idem
31. MacKillop, p. 108
32. Smyth, p. 22-23
33. Loc Cit
34. Ibid, p. 125-127
35. MacKillop, p. , p. 109-110
36. Idem
37. Green, Dictionary, p. 69, 174
38. Ibid, p.
39. Carmichael, p. 618
40. Kondratiev, Apple Branch, p. 81, 87-88, 259
41. Kondratiev, Basic Celtic Deity Types
42. Briggs, Encyclopedia, p. 58-59
43. Green, Dictionary, p. 107
44. This is my own extension of material found in many works, including Ibid, p. 120-122
45. Kondratiev, Apple Branch, p. 81, 88-89, 259
46. Op Cit, p. 194-195
47. Idem

48. Kondratiev, Apple Branch, p. 82, 89-90, 260
49. Op Cit, p. 203-204
50. Medieval Ireland: the Enduring Tradition/ Michael Richter, with a foreword by Próinséas ni Caitháin – New York: St. Martin's, c1983, 1988, p. 15, 17-22
51. MacKillop, p. 414
52. This is my own reconstruction, based on sources cited in this chapter
53. Also my own reconstruction
54. Cattle lords and clansmen: the social structure of early Ireland/ Nerys Thomas Patterson – Notre Dame, IN: University of Notre Dame Press, c1994 – 2nd edition, pp. 29, 173, 194-195, 239-242.
55. Ibid, p. 239-258
56. Ó Tuathail, p. 14
57. A handbook of the Scottish Gaelic world/ Michael Newton – [Dublin]: Four Courts Press, c2000, p.118-121
58. Ibid, p. 118-121, 139
59. Patterson, p. 251-258
60. Idem
61. Richter, p. 20-22
62. This is my own list, mostly taken from:` A social history of ancient Ireland: manners, customs, and domestic life of the ancient Irish/ PW Joyce – [s/l]: Irish Genealogical Foundation – 2nd edition – 1997
63. Aes Dana ranks taken from: The Druids/ Peter Berrisford Ellis – Grand Rapids, MI: William Eerdman's, c1994 p. 157-162, but modified for modern use. Other ranks taken from Patterson, 181-206, 366-367, but *greatly* modified for modern use, and influenced by PW Joyce.
64. Patterson, p. 207-223
65. Ibid, p. 155-161
66. Ibid, p. 161-180
67. Sex and marriage in ancient Ireland/ Patrick C. Power – [Dublin]: Mercier, c1976 p. 25
68. Ibid, p. 30-31
69. Idem
70. Ibid, p. 25-32
71. Rees and Rees, p. 259-267
72. Ibid, p. 267-271
73. Lady with a mead cup: ritual, prophecy, and lordship in the European warband from LaTene to the Viking Age/ Michael J. Enright – [Dublin]: Four Courts, c1996 p. 262-268

74. Patterson, p. 294-296
75. Idem
76. Idem
77. Idem
78. Idem
79. Idem
80. Ó Tuathail, p. 2
81. Joyce, p.
82. Celtic Law: a short summary: part 1-12/ Raimund Karl (a870035@uNéit.univie.ac.at) – Celtic culture mailing list (CelticL@Danann.hea.ie), c1990-1997
83. Idem
84. Idem
85. Idem
86. Idem
87. Idem
88. Idem

## Notes to Chapter 4

1. Rees and Rees, p. 297, 314
2. Smyth, p. 144-148
3. Fire in the head: shamanism and the Celtic spirit/ Tom Cowan – San Francisco: HarperSanFrancisco, c1993, p. 206-208
4. A Druid herbal for the sacred Earth year/ Ellen Evert Hopman – Rochester, VT: Destiny Books, 1995, p. 148-151
5. This is my interpretation. The concept of an *exemplary model* is used by Rees and Rees to describe the mythic narrative on p. 104-107.
6. Loc Cit
7. Idem, also Briggs, Encyclopedia, p. 290-294 on Merrows
8. Rees and Rees, p. 40-41
9. This is my own interpretation of the above
10. Rees and Rees, p. 297-301
11. Stewart, Robert Kirk, p. 138-142
12. This is my own interpretation
13. Smyth, p. 87-88
14. Stewart, Robert Kirk, p. 141-150
15. See the description of Manannán in Chapter 2
16. Smyth, p. 87-88
17. Idem
18. Ibid, p. 86-91

19. Stewart, Robert Kirk, p. 141
20. This is my own interpretation
21. Rees and Rees, p. 316-325
22. Stewart, Robert Kirk, p. 142
23. Lincoln, p. 119-120
24. Ibid, p. 23-29
25. Idem
26. Idem
27. Ó Tuathail p.13
28. The Fairy Faith in Celtic countries/ WY Evans-Wentz – [New York]: Citadel, c1966 – introduction, c1990 p. 339
29. Smyth, p. 77
30. Sjoestedt, p. 66
31. Rees and Rees, p. 299
32. Imram Brain, quoted by Lincoln, p. 24
33. Smyth, p. 144-148
34. Idem
35. Lincoln, p. 28-29 on inexhaustible light in Otherworld tales. Recollections of death: a medical investigation/ Michael B. Sabom – New York: Harper & Row, c1982, p. 44 on Near Death Experiences.
36. Smyth, p. 139-140
37. Lincoln, p. 25
38. Cowan, p. 76-79
39. Ibid, p. 79-81
40. Ibid, p. 76-79
41. Smyth, p. 144-148
42. Lincoln, p. 24
43. Briggs, Vanishing People, p. 100
44. Smyth, p. 80-82
45. Smyth, p. 87-88
46. Briggs, Encyclopedia, p. 310-312
47. Smyth, p. 89-90
1. Rees and Rees, p. 310-312

## Notes to Chapter 5

1. Smyth, p. 74, for "under sea". Epstein, p. 74-75 for "demons/evil spirits".
2. Briggs, Encyclopedia, p. 129-130.

3. Cath Maige Tuired, p.
4. Kondratiev, Apple Branch, p. 184-186
5. Idem
6. Focloir Draiochta, p. 14
7. Foclóir Gaelige-Béarla, p. 433-434
8. This is my own interpretation
9. Celtic myth and legend, poetry and romance / by Charles Squire: with illustrations after paintings by IHF Bacon, ARA, and other artists – [Van Nuys, CA]: Newcastle Publishing, c1975 p. 270-271
10. Rees and Rees p. 298-303
11. Smyth, p. 58-59
12. Rees and Rees, p. 303
13. Ibid, p. 142
14. The Táin/ translated from the Irish epic Táin Bó Cualigne by Thomas Kinsella: with brush drawings by Louis le Brocquy – Oxford: Oxford University Press, c1969, 1970 p. 25-45
15. Rees and Rees, p. 303, also
16. The Silver Bough: volume 1: Scottish folk-lore and folk-belief / F. Marian McNeill: introduced by Stewart Sanderson – Edinburgh: Canongate Classics, c1956, 1989 p. 77-78
17. Idem
18. Briggs, Encyclopedia, p. 335-336
19. Idem
20. Idem
21. Idem
22. Ibid, p. 74-75
23. Ibid, p. 30-32
24. Ibid, p. 43
25. Ibid, p. 129-130
26. Ibid, p. 182
27. Ibid, p.373-374

## Notes to Chapter 6

1. Foclóir Gaelige-Béarla, p. 715
2. Ó Tuathail, p. 14
3. The world of the Celts/ Simon James – [New York]: Thames and Hudson, c1993 p. 92-95
4. Idem
5. Idem
6. Idem

7. Green, Dictionary, p. 127-129
8. Kondratiev, Apple Branch, p. 78-82
9. Idem
10. Ellis, p. 162
11. Loc Cit
12. Idem
13. This is a well-known part of Highland dress
14. This is well-known as a article of Iron-age Celtic jewelry
15. MacCrossan, p. 110
16. Idem
17. Ó Tuathail p. 5
18. Carmichael, p. 292
19. Ibid, p. 289
20. Ibid, p.296
21. Ibid, p.293-294
22. Ibid, p. 81
23. Ibid, p. 84-85
24. Ibid, p. 87-88

## Notes to Chapter 7

2. The Druids/ Stuart Piggott – [New York]: Thames and Hudson, c1968, 1975, p. 113-115
3. Rees and Rees, p. 97-98
4. Idem, also Lincoln, p. 33-36
5. Lincoln, p. 32-48 on the Indo-European origins of the myth of Donn, and p. 23-31 on the Otherworld concept itself, including associations with the dead.
6. Evans-Wentz, p. 68
7. Briggs, Encyclopedia, p. 373-374
8. Ó Tuathail, p. 2
9. Evans-Wentz, p. 370-373
10. Smyth, p. 117-118
11. Evans-Wentz, p. 385
12. This is my own interpretation
13. Foclóir Gaelige-Béarla, p.1192
14. Ibid, p. 44
15. Briggs, Encyclopedia, p.14-16
16. Ibid, p. 29
17. Ibid, p. 19-20

# Bibliography

An encyclopedia of fairies: hobogoblins, brownies, bogies, and other supernatural creatures / Katherine Briggs – New York: Pantheon, c1976

The vanishing people: Fairy lore and legends/ Katherine Briggs, illustrations by Mary French – New York, Pantheon c1978

Carmina Gadelica: hymns and incantations,: with illustrative notes on wards, rites, and customs dying and obsolete/ orally collected in the Highlands and Islands of Scotland by Alexander Carmichael – [Hudson, NY]: Lindisfarne, c1992 (republication)

Cath Maige Tuired: the 2nd Battle of Mag Tuired/ edited by Elizabeth A. Gray – Dublin: Irish Texts Society, 1982

University of Wales Center for Advanced Welsh and Celtic Studies – Celtic lexicon – http://www.aber.ac.uk/~awcwww/PCI_MoE.pdf

Fire in the head: shamanism and the Celtic spirit/ Tom Cowan – San Francisco: HarperSanFrancisco, c1993

The Year in Ireland/ by Kevin Dánaher – [Dublin]: Mercier, c1972

Poems from the Dindsenchas: text, translation, and vocabulary – Royal Irish Academy Todd Lecture Series, Vol. II/ by Edward Gwynne – Dublin: Academy House, 1900

Lady with a mead cup: ritual, prophecy, and lordship in the European warband from LaTene to the Viking Age/ Michael J. Enright – [Dublin]: Four Courts, c1996

War Goddess: the Morrígan and her Germano-Celtic counterparts / by Angelique Gulermovich Epstein – Los Angeles: University of California Los Angeles, 1998

The Fairy Faith in Celtic countries/ WY Evans-Wentz – [New York]: Citadel, c1966 – introduction, c1990

Dictionary of Celtic myth and legend/ Miranda J. Green – [New York]: Thames and Hudson, c1992

Lugus/ Christopher Gwinn – copyright, 2000 Christopher Gwinn. Internet document, no longer extant to my knowledge.

The world of the Celts/ Simon James – [New York]: Thames and Hudson, c1993

A social history of ancient Ireland: manners, customs, and domestic life of the ancient Irish/ PW Joyce – [s/l]: Irish Genealogical Foundation – 2$^{nd}$ edition – 1997

"*butācos, *u̯ossos, *gei̯stlos, *ambaātos: Celtic socio-economic organization in the European Iron Age"/ Mag. Dr. Raimund Karl – paper presented to the Cerrig Milltir – Milestones Conference at the University of Wales Centre of Advanced Welsh and Celtic Studies, Aberystwyth, 1/7/2005, later slightly modified and published on the interet, [2007].

Celtic Law: a short summary: part 1-12/ Raimund Karl (a870035@uNet.univie.ac.at) – Celtic culture mailing list (CelticL@Danann.hea.ie), c1990-1997

The Apple Branch: a path to Celtic ritual/ Alexei Kondratiev – [Cork, Ireland: Collins Press], c1998

Basic Celtic Deity Types/ Alexei Kondratiev - copyright and copy, 1997 Alexei Kondratiev. Internet document, no longer extant to my knowledge.

Celtic Values/ Alexei Kondratiev – internet document. This is from an earlier version (ca. 1995) than the one currently widely available on the internet.

"Dánu and Bile: the primordial parents?" / Alexei Kondratiev: An Tríbhís Mhór, vol. 1, no. 2 – Montague, NJ: Imbas, Bealtaine, 1998

"Lugus: the Many Skilled Lord"/ Alexei Kondratiev – internet document.

Labarion-English Dictionary – http://p3.grp.yahoofs.com/v1/cPBtQONetum

Irish Texts Society, v. XXXIX Lebor Gabála Érenn:, part III/ edited and translated by RAS Macallister – Dublin: Irish Texts Society, 1941

Irish Texts Society, vol. XLI Lebor Gabála Érenn: part 4 / edited and translated by RAS Macallister – Dublin, 1941

Death, war, and sacrifice: studies in ideology and practice/ Bruce Lincoln; forward by Wendy Doniger – Chicago: University of Chicago Press, c1991

The sacred cauldron: secrets of the Druids/ Tadhg MacCrossan – St. Paul, MN: Llewellyn, 1991

A dictionary of Celtic mythology / James MacKillop – [Oxford]: Oxford University Press, c1998

A handbook of the Scottish Gaelic world/ Michael Newton – [Dublin]: Four Courts Press, c2000

Foclóir Gaelige-Béarla / Niall Ó Dónaill – [Baile Átha Cliath]: An Gúm, c1977, 1992

Foclóir Draíochta – Dictionary of Druidism/ by Sean Ó Tuathail – copyright 1993 John Kellnhauser/Cainteanna na Luise

Cattle lords and clansmen: the social structure of early Ireland/ Nerys Thomas Patterson – Notre Dame, IN: University of Notre Dame Press, c1994 – 2nd edition

Sex and marriage in ancient Ireland/ Patrick C. Power – [Dublin]: Mercier, c1976

Celtic heritage: ancient tradition in Ireland and Wales/ Alwyn and Brinley Rees – [New York]: Thames and Hudson, c1961

Medieval Ireland: the Enduring Tradition/ Michael Richter, with a foreword by Próinséas ni Caitháin – New York: St. Martin's, c1983, 1988

Recollections of death: a medical investigation/ Michale B. Sabom – New York: Harper & Row, c1982, p. 44 on Near Death Experiences.

Gods and heroes of the Celts/ Marie-Louise Sjoestedt, translated by Myles Dillon – Berekley, CA: Turtle Island Foundation, 1982

A guide to Irish mythology / Daragh Smyth – [Dublin]: Irish Academic, c1988, 1996

Celtic Gods, Celtic Goddesses/ RJ Stewart, illustrated by Miranda Grey and Courtney Davis – [London]: Blandford, c1990

Earth light: the ancient path to transformation: rediscovering the wisdom of ancient Celtic and Faerie lore/ RJ Stewart – Rockport, MA: Element, c1992

Robert Kirk: walker between worlds: a new edition of the secret commonwealth of elves, fauns, and fairies/ RJ Stewart – Shaftesbury, Dorset: Element Books, c1990

Irish Texts Society, v. XLIX Táin Bo Cúaligne/ edited by Cecile O'Rahilly – Dublin: Irish Texts Society, 1967

Printed in the United States
134604LV00002B/350/P